# AMERICA'S
# ELECTRIC
# UTILITIES

# AMERICA'S ELECTRIC UTILITIES

## Under Siege and in Transition

### Scott Fenn

PRAEGER SPECIAL STUDIES • PRAEGER SCIENTIFIC

New York • Philadelphia • Eastbourne, UK
Toronto • Hong Kong • Tokyo • Sydney

Library of Congress Cataloging in Publication Data

Fenn, Scott.
    America's electric utilities.

    Includes bibliographical references.
    1. Electric utilities—United States.  I. Title.
HD9685.U5F434   1984            363.6'2         84-8279
ISBN 0-03-070301-8 (alk. paper)

Published in 1984 by Praeger Publishers
CBS Educational and Professional Publishing,
a Division of CBS Inc.
521 Fifth Avenue, New York, NY 10175 USA

456789  052  9876545321

Printed in the United States of America
on acid-free paper

To my grandparents,

Ted and Lucille Bolton

# PREFACE

Throughout the past decade, the electric utility industry has confronted major changes in its operating environment that have weakened its financial condition and stunted its growth. Many of these changes were of an economic nature, such as the rapid rise in interest rates and fuel prices. Others involved political factors, such as the growing opposition to nuclear generating stations and increasing politicization of the ratemaking process. These events have forced the industry into a period of transition to new technologies and new business strategies.

A continuing uncertainty facing the industry relates to public acceptance of the conventional generating technologies traditionally favored by utility planners--large central-station nuclear and coal-fired plants. The problems plaguing nuclear power development have brought a six year moratorium on new orders and show few signs of easing. More recently, growing concern over the externalities associated with burning coal have raised serious questions about the cost and environmental consequences of new coal plant construction.

At the same time, rising utility rates have provoked consumers' ire and calls for greater consumer input into utility regulation. Moreover, the prospect of increased competition from decentralized generating sources has spawned support for deregulation of electric generation and prompted some utilities to explore diversification outside of the regulated utility business.

Concerns such as these have radically altered the concept of utility planning by infusing discussion of technical and economic issues with questions of political viability and corporate social responsibility. It was through its interest in these types of questions that the Investor Responsibility Research Center (IRRC) became involved in research on electric utilities.

IRRC was founded in 1972 by a number of universities and foundations seeking impartial reporting on a variety of public policy and corporate responsibility issues, particularly those issues raised in shareholder proposals at corporate annual meetings. The Center now provides research and reporting to more than 160 institutional investors on a variety of issues relating to the role of business in society.

One focus of IRRC's work in recent years has been energy issues. The Center has published two books on the debate over nuclear power development, as well as studies on industrial energy conservation, factors affecting future coal use, and electric utility load management and alternative energy programs. In 1981, IRRC undertook a study to synthesize the issues affecting the future of America's electric utilities. The Center published its initial report in 1983 and updated it extensively to provide the basis for this book.

This book is designed to provide readers with a basic understanding of the pressures confronting the electric utility industry, the industry's response to these pressures and the implications of these developments for energy users, investors and consumers. The focus of the book is on where the industry is going, not where it has been. It is not meant to pass judgment on particular energy technologies or corporate strategies, which are likely to continue to undergo dramatic changes in the years ahead.

# ACKNOWLEDGEMENTS

I owe a debt of gratitude to many people for their help and encouragement in completing this study. Special thanks are due to IRRC and its executive director, Margaret Carroll; to Carolyn Mathiasen for her clear thinking and sage counsel in editing my drafts; and to Shirley Carpenter for her tireless assistance in preparing this manuscript for publication.

While I accept full responsibility for the interpretations of data and conclusions contained in this study, I gratefully acknowledge a number of reviewers for their insightful comments on an earlier version of this book. I thank especially Desaix Myers III of the U.S. Agency for International Development; Robert Spann of ICF, Inc.; Robert Malko and Gregory Enholm of the Wisconsin Public Service Commission; and Douglas Cogan of IRRC for their criticisms and contributions to my thinking.

Lucien Smartt of Public Utilities Reports, Alvin Kaufman of the Congressional Research Service, Michael Foley of the National Association of Regulatory Utility Commissioners, Charles Komanoff of Komanoff Energy Associates, Mason Willrich of Pacific Gas & Electric, Peter Hunt of Peter Hunt Associates, Amory Lovins of the Rocky Mountain Institute, Christopher Flavin of Worldwatch Institute and Milton Searl of the Electric Power Research Institute also provided valuable oral or written comments.

Finally, I thank Carole Robertson and my friends and family for their encouragement and support of my passion for putting words on paper.

S.A.F.

# CONTENTS

# LIST OF TABLES

# LIST OF FIGURES

# I
# INTRODUCTION

Over the last decade, energy policy decisionmakers in the United States have focused attention on first one fuel source, then another, as the country has lurched between energy crises. The oil embargo of 1973, the natural gas shortage in the winter of 1976-77, the United Mine Workers' strike of 1977-78, the Iranian oil shock and Three Mile Island nuclear mishap of 1979, and the natural gas price runup of 1982 all attracted considerable attention and activity from government policymakers. Through it all, however, U.S. energy policy has failed to grapple with one of the most important long-range questions concerning the nation's energy future--the future of the electric power sector.

Energy policy stands at the center of three critical and sometimes conflicting national concerns—economic growth, environmental quality and national security. To a greater extent than any other industry, the electric utility industry is the nexus of these concerns. The industry's strategic position guarantees that it is only a matter of time before it occupies the center stage in the debate over energy policy in the United States. Government economic and tax policies, along with safety and environmental regulations, will profoundly affect the economic prospects and management strategies of the utility industry. Likewise, decisions made by the industry will have enormous ramifications for the options available to government policymakers and the general quality of life for the population at large, affecting everything from the cleanliness of the air we breathe to the price of running a computer.

A major public policy debate over future electric power needs and policy is already raging. This controversy has tended to pit electric utilities, the federal government and other supporters of conventional electricity supply options against consumers, environmentalists and, to a limited extent, regulators searching for more cost-effective or environmentally benign alternatives. At the same time, however, regional economic and political differences have begun to fracture the unity of the electric utility industry's position on many aspects of the debate, yielding utility executives with opposing views on many basic issues.

The debate over the role electricity will play in the nation's energy future is not likely to be resolved soon. The issues involved are complex and the stakes are enormous. Neither side is likely to be swayed from its position until that position becomes indefensible--a process that could take a decade or more. Electric utilities, however, are not likely to have the luxury of waiting until the academic debate is resolved before they must commit themselves to business decisions based on their perception of future energy trends.

Poised on the threshold of these decisions, the industry finds itself adrift in a world in which most of the assumptions on which it has based its planning have turned topsy-turvy. Over the last decade, skyrocketing fuel prices, escalating power plant construction costs, inflation and high interest rates, stagnant growth in demand, intractable public doubt about the safety of nuclear power, and now, growing awareness of the serious harmful effects of burning coal have introduced a wealth of uncertainties to what was once a highly predictable industry. In the process, these forces have also transformed scores of America's blue chip companies into financial basket cases. The pressures and uncertainties facing electric utilities are forcing them to reexamine every aspect of their business--the types of energy they will produce, the technologies they will use, the effort and expenditures they will devote to conservation and demand management programs, the extent to which they will diversify out of the electric power business, and the methods they will use to maintain financial integrity.

The decade of the 1980s will be critical for America's electric utilities as they reassess their views of the political and economic environment they must operate in and grope for new business strategies that offer the most promise for future success. The entire structure of the industry is likely to change within a decade, and its new form will be determined largely by the industry's reaction to growing outside pressures for change. The industry is likely to remain heavily regulated, yet increasingly it will also be subject to competition. For many companies, this new era will offer business opportunities far beyond the scope of traditional utility operations. On the other hand, some companies that are unable to respond to the economic and political maelstrom now confronting the industry are not likely to be around long enough to see the new power plants now on their drawing boards serve out their estimated lifespans. More important, the business strategies that utilities adopt will profoundly influence the competitiveness of American industry, perceptions of our national security, and the quality of the natural environment for decades to come. Specifically, the topic of this book is of fundamental importance to investors and society for the following reasons:

- Electric power availability and prices have an enormous impact on a wide range of important industries, from aluminum and steel production to the industries that many economists regard as the best hope for U.S. economic revitalization-- electronics, computers and robotics.

- Power plant emissions may well be the single most important factor affecting the future quality of the environment in the United States. Radiation levels at various points in the nuclear fuel cycle, sulfur dioxide and small particulate levels in the air, and growing concerns about acid rain, carbon dioxide buildup in the atmosphere and the availability of clean water in the West, all hinge on decisions made by the utility industry and its regulators.

- Decisions by utility officials could have important implications for national security, especially on matters pertaining to the proliferation of nuclear technology, the vulnerability of U.S. energy supplies to disruption or sabotage, and the assurance of sufficient energy supplies to meet national needs.

- The electric utility industry is the most capital-intensive in the nation, accounting for one-fifth of all new industrial construction, one-third of all corporate financing, and one-half of all new common stock issuances among industrial companies. Thus, the industry's financial condition has broad implications for the stability of capital markets, the price and availability of capital to other industries, and the economy.

- Electric utilities are the largest consumer of primary energy in the economy, accounting for about one-third of total primary energy demand. Industry decisions about generating technologies will greatly influence the kinds of energy options available to consumers in the future, as well as their cost.

- Interest group, consumer and regulatory activism concerning electric utilities continues to grow. Ratepayers' outrage over rising electricity rates portends continued politicization of the rate-making process. Congressional action on deregulation in the natural gas and telephone industries, which have a number of similarities to the electric power industry, suggest future changes in the major legislation governing electric utilities.

This study examines the electric utility industry at this critical juncture. It looks at the nature and sources of the pressures facing the industry and the evolving business strategies that various electric utilities are implementing in response. Chapter II discusses the role of the electric utility industry in the energy economy and outlines the industry's development. Chapter III examines the political, financial and social pressures confronting electric utilities and the new perceptions about the industry's business environment that these pressures have imposed on utility planners. Chapter IV looks at the divergent business strategies that utilities are implementing in response to these changes in their business environment and at their rationales for these strategies. Chapter V explores various proposals for changes in utility regulation and their chances for passage. Chapter VI contains the author's summary and conclusions.

# II
# ELECTRIC UTILITIES
# AND
# THE ENERGY ECONOMY

## Energy and Electricity

Electric utilities occupy a special niche in the U.S. energy economy. Typically, they are neither energy producers--like oil or coal mining companies--nor end-use consumers such as individual homeowners, commercial buildings or factories. Yet they consume and produce vast quantities of energy in their role as a converter of energy from one form to another and as energy distributors. In 1982, for instance, electric utilities accounted for 84 percent of the nation's coal consumption and supplied about 10 percent of the country's total energy demand. They did so by taking energy from primary sources--oil, gas, coal, uranium and falling water--converting it to electricity in large nuclear, hydroelectric or fossil-fueled central generating stations, and then sending it out to consumers through vast networks of transmission lines.

This conversion and distribution process is not particularly efficient in terms of physics; some 65 to 70 percent of the energy present in the primary fuel is now lost in conversion and distribution. But electricity is an attractive energy source, nevertheless, because it is clean, it can be transported almost instantaneously over great distances, and it is extremely versatile in its uses. While electricity competes with other more efficent energy forms for end-use applications such as heating, there are a number of basic processes for which it is crucial--including lighting, mechanical drive, telecommunications and electronics. As a result, demand for electricity has grown historically at a rapid pace and, even recently, as total energy demand growth has slackened, electricity demand has continued to increase as a percentage of total energy demand.

The uniqueness of the electric utility industry is not confined to the economic sphere--it is unique in its political role as well. Because of the extremely capital-intensive nature of the business, the industry is considered a natural monopoly. Utilities therefore have been granted monopoly franchises on a geographical basis, in exchange for which they are obligated to meet all the power requirements of consumers within that area, and their rates are subject to government regulation. The industry's obligation to serve all customers has generally required that utilities plan conservatively for the future, maintaining at least a 20 percent reserve margin of capacity and setting up power pools to ensure that power supplies will always be available when needed. Meanwhile, government regulatory involvement has evolved in the form of state public utility commissions whose members are elected or appointed by state governors. Thus, the economic context in which utilities operate is colored by political and social considerations to a far greater extent than is true for most industries.

Historical background: The electric utility industry in the United States was born in 1882 and developed along a vertically integrated path envisioned by Thomas Edison and others. The industry's early years were rather confused as local companies competed for nonexclusive franchises, with some selling DC (direct current) power and others selling AC (alternating current) power. Beginning around 1900, however, utilities began organizing into mammoth holding companies and AC power became dominant, largely because it could be transported for greater distances. The total number of operating companies peaked by about 1917. From this point on, central station electric generation achieved ever greater penetration of the electricity market, rising from 40 percent of all power supplies at the turn of the century to 80 percent by the early 1930s. By 1932, 16 holding companies controlled operating companies that generated more than 75 percent of the nation's power.

The present structure of the industry began to take shape in the period between the Depression and World War II with the breakup of the utility holding companies and the merger of many small operating companies. In the 20 years following the passage of the Public Utility Holding Company Act of 1935--a piece of New Deal legislation designed to correct the abuses of utility holding companies by dismembering them--more than 700 companies were split off from utility holding companies and the number of holding companies fell from several hundred to 18.

Following World War II, electric utilities entered into a golden age of declining costs and prices, satisfied customers, investors and regulators and steady growth. Electricity demand growth was vigorous and predictable, with electric power usage growing at a compound annual rate of 7.8 percent and peak load growth averaging 8.1 percent a year between 1945 and 1970. 1/ The life of a postwar utility planner was so simple that some observers joked that the only tool needed to forecast electricity demand growth was "a good ruler." During this period, electricity demand growth resulted from two powerful forces: (1) overall growth in energy demand, spurred in part by declining real energy prices; and (2) a trend toward greater use of electricity relative to other forms of energy because of electricity's convenience, versatility and declining relative price.

The golden age for electric utilities appears to have peaked in the mid-1960s. Utility stock prices and mortgage bond interest coverage ratios both reached all-time highs in 1965. In the same year, however, an equipment failure at an Ontario Hydro station plunged 30 million people throughout the northeastern United States into a blackout, providing a harbinger of future problems for the industry. By the time of the Arab oil embargo of 1973, the world of the electric utility planner had turned upside down. Rising oil prices, interest rates and construction costs increased utility costs faster than revenues and transformed the industry from a decreasing cost to an increasing cost business. As prices for virtually all forms of energy began to rise dramatically in the 1970s, consumers started to cut back on energy consumption wherever possible. Growth in total energy demand--which had been averaging 3 percent a year for several decades--slumped to near zero. In fact, total domestic energy consumption in 1982 was 70.9 quadrillion Btu (quads), about 5 percent below the country's level of consumption in 1973. 2/ Meanwhile, electricity sales and peak demand growth fell to less than one-third of their previous levels. Since 1973, electricity sales growth has averaged 2.2 percent a year while peak demand growth has averaged 2.3 percent.

The sharp drop in peak demand and sales growth since 1973 caught most electric utilities off guard. Initially, they assumed that any fall-off in demand growth would be short-lived and continued to order new generating plants. Later, they began to scale back their estimates of future demand growth, but their downward revisions were inevitably too optimistic. As shown in Figure 1, the industry has cut its projections of peak demand growth every year since 1974. As a result, surplus generating capacity for the industry as a whole --which the industry attempts to maintain at a 20 percent level-- climbed from 21 percent in 1973 to 31 percent in 1977, and then to almost 40 percent at the end of 1982--the highest level since 1938. 3/

Electricity's growing role: The decline in electricity demand growth since 1973 has tended to obscure an important fact: Consumers have continued to see electricity as the energy of choice. Electricity's role in the overall energy economy kept growing throughout the 1970s, continuing a trend that has been in progress since the 1920s. As Table 1 shows, while total energy consumption fell slightly between 1973 and 1982, the electric utility industry boosted its portion from about a quarter of total energy consumption at the time of the Arab oil embargo to more than one-third of total energy consumption today. Moreover, this ratio of energy consumption by electric utilities to total energy consumption has risen steadily through periods of recession as well as those of vigorous economic growth. Thus, although one of the two traditional sources of electricity demand growth--growth in overall energy demand--has ceased to exist since

Figure 1.

## Projected Peak Demand

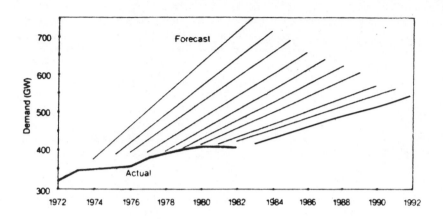

SOURCE:  National Electric Reliability Council data.

1973, the other--substitution of electric power for other end-use energy forms--has continued as consumers have switched to electricity from other energy sources.

## The Structure of the Electric Utility Industry

The electric utility industry consists of about 3,000 companies that supply electricity to more than 92 million households, commercial establishments and industrial operations. The industry is composed of four distinct ownership segments--investor-owned corporations; public systems owned by the federal government; public systems owned by states, municipalities, or utility districts; and cooperatives. The statistics on page 11 provide an overview of the industry's development in several areas.

Investor-owned utilities:  About 200 investor-owned electric utilities dominate the industry, generating 78 percent of the country's power and supplying 76 percent of all retail customers. 4/  These private companies are an assimilation of some 2,000 private utility systems that were in existence in the 1920s. Actual control of the industry is even more centralized because a number of utility holding companies own up to seven operating utilities and because the largest private systems account for most of this segment's generating capacity. Table 2 shows the 10 largest investor-owned systems in terms of assets.

Table 1.

### Primary Energy Consumption by Electric Utilities

| Year | Domestic energy consumption (quads) | Primary energy inputs electric utilities (quads) | % of total consumption |
|------|------|------|------|
| 1970 | 66.83 | 16.29 | 24.4 |
| 1971 | 68.30 | 17.22 | 25.2 |
| 1972 | 71.63 | 18.58 | 25.9 |
| 1973 | 74.61 | 19.85 | 26.6 |
| 1974 | 72.76 | 20.02 | 27.5 |
| 1975 | 70.71 | 20.35 | 28.8 |
| 1976 | 74.51 | 21.57 | 28.9 |
| 1977 | 76.33 | 22.69 | 29.7 |
| 1978 | 78.18 | 23.72 | 30.3 |
| 1979 | 78.91 | 24.07 | 30.5 |
| 1980 | 75.99 | 24.50 | 32.2 |
| 1981 | 73.98 | 24.68 | 33.4 |
| 1982 | 70.89 | 24.15 | 34.1 |

SOURCE: Energy Information Administration, Monthly Energy Review, September 1983.

Federal systems: Power generated from federal dams and installations is marketed through six federal agencies--Bonneville Power Administration, Southeastern Power Administration, Southwestern Power Administration, Alaska Power Administration, the Bureau of Reclamation and the Tennessee Valley Authority. The first five of these systems are operated by the Department of the Interior and have traditionally served as marketers of power from federal hydroelectric projects, although they are now developing other energy sources as well. The Tennessee Valley Authority was established in 1933 as an autonomous agency to promote the development of the Tennessee River Basin and has grown to become the largest electric power producer in the country, operating nuclear and fossil-fueled plants as well as hydroelectric facilities. The idea behind the formation of TVA and other government-owned utilities was that they could serve as a yardstick by which to measure the performance of private utilities.

Together, the six federal systems have an installed generating capacity of 62,544 megawatts, accounting for about 9.6 percent of the country's generating capacity in 1982. 5/ All federal systems

Table 2.

## Ten Largest Investor-owned Electric Utilities, 1982

| System | Assets | Operating Revenues |
|--------|--------|-------------------|
|        | (millions) | (millions) |
| Pacific Gas & Electric | 13,635.3 | 6,785.1 |
| Commonwealth Edison | 12,582.0 | 4,129.7 |
| Southern Co. | 12,301.2 | 4,927.2 |
| American Electric Power | 12,223.8 | 4,180.0 |
| Middle South Utilities | 10,364.7 | 2,901.7 |
| Southern California Edison | 10,157.6 | 4,302.6 |
| Texas Utilities | 8,021.4 | 3,238.0 |
| Public Service Elec. & Gas | 7,907.0 | 3,874.0 |
| Consolidated Edison | 7,872.1 | 5,067.4 |
| Detroit Edison | 7,635.7 | 2,123.3 |

SOURCE: Fortune, June 13, 1983

are required to give preference in the sale of their power output to other public systems and cooperatives and much of the output from these systems is sold at wholesale rates.

Other public systems: In addition to the large federal systems, there are about 2,200 municipal, state and regional public power systems ranging in size from tiny municipal power distributors to giant publicly owned systems like the Power Authority of the State of New York, the Washington Public Power Supply System and the Salt River Project in Arizona. Muncipal systems—such as those in Los Angeles and Seattle—are usually run by the local city council or an independent board elected by voters or appointed by city officials. Other public systems are run by public utility districts, irrigation districts or special state authorities.

Together, municipal, state and regional public power systems generate about 9 percent of the nation's electricity but account for about 15 percent of total electricity sales. This discrepancy results from the fact that many municipal and regional electric systems are involved in electric power distribution only and purchase power from private or federal electric utilities for resale to consumers. Most publicly owned utilities are not required to pay state and local taxes and are exempt from federal income taxes, which has tended to spur their growth in recent years.

# U.S. ELECTRIC UTILITY STATISTICS

Table 3.

| Year | Electric Operating Revenues (millions of dollars) | | | kWh Sales to Ultimate Customers | | | | Number of Ultimate Customers | | | |
|------|------|------|------|------|------|------|------|------|------|------|------|
| | Local Public | Rural Co-Op | Private | Total Sales (million kwh) | Local Public | Rural Co-Op | Private | Total (millions) | Local Public | Rural Co-Op | Private |
| 1982 | $16,747 | $13,982 | $109,961 | 2,058,479 | 15.0% | 7.4% | 77.6% | 95,676 | 13.4% | 10.6% | 76.1% |
| 1981 | 14,378 | 11,795 | 102,301 | 2,103,529 | 15.2 | 7.1 | 77.7 | 94,448 | 13.5 | 10.4 | 76.1 |
| 1980 | 12,224 | 9,707 | 87,062 | 2,082,010 | 15.2 | 7.0 | 77.8 | 92,612 | 13.5 | 10.2 | 76.3 |
| 1979 | 9,946 | 8,061 | 72,851 | 2,004,828 | 13.0 | 7.0 | 80.1 | 90,806 | 13.7 | 10.2 | 76.1 |
| 1978 | 8,732 | 7,038 | 65,427 | 1,941,849 | 12.7 | 6.8 | 80.5 | 88,150 | 13.6 | 10.2 | 76.2 |
| 1977 | 7,654 | 5,802 | 58,865 | 1,868,267 | 12.6 | 5.7 | 80.7 | 85,997 | 13.5 | 10.0 | 76.4 |
| 1976 | 6,536 | 4,725 | 50,552 | 1,761,857 | 12.9 | 5.7 | 80.5 | 84,214 | 13.5 | 9.9 | 76.7 |
| 1975 | 5,612 | 3,887 | 44,558 | 1,676,548 | 12.9 | 6.4 | 80.7 | 82,616 | 13.5 | 9.7 | 76.8 |
| 1970 | 3,175 | 1,535 | 19,791 | 1,341,293 | 14.1 | 5.1 | 80.7 | 72,914 | 13.6 | 8.8 | 77.6 |
| 1965 | 2,295 | 938 | 13,430 | 905,462 | 14.8 | 4.5 | 80.7 | 65,752 | 13.6 | 8.4 | 78.0 |
| 1960 | 1,368 | 615 | 10,116 | 636,433 | 14.2 | 4.3 | 81.5 | 59,711 | 13.1 | 8.1 | 78.8 |
| 1955 | 937 | 420 | 7,199 | 447,199 | 13.5 | 3.5 | 82.9 | 52,556 | 13.0 | 8.0 | 79.0 |
| 1950 | 618 | 229 | 4,734 | 278,302 | 13.1 | 2.5 | 84.4 | 44,223 | 12.8 | 7.7 | 79.5 |
| 1947 | 457 | 111 | 3,697 | 214,964 | 12.6 | 1.4 | 86.0 | 37,373 | 12.6 | 5.5 | 81.9 |
| 1937 | 155 | -- | 2,158 | 97,686 | 5.8 | -- | 94.2 | 26,243 | 10.1 | 0.2 | 89.7 |
| 1927 | 122 | -- | 1,680 | 79,012 | 4.6 | -- | 95.4 | 21,786 | 9.8 | -- | 90.2 |
| 1917 | 40 | -- | 462 | 25,752 | 4.0 | -- | 96.0 | 7,179 | 13.6 | -- | 86.4 |

NOTE: This table excludes federal power systems.

SOURCE: Statistics compiled by the American Public Power Association, the Energy Information Administration and the Rural Electrification Administration as reported in Public Power.

Electric cooperatives: Electric cooperatives are an outgrowth of government efforts to promote the use of electricity in rural areas. Congress created the Rural Electrification Administration in 1935 and subsequently gave it broad lending authority to stimulate rural electrification. Rural co-ops are owned by their customers, each of whom has one vote in the election of a board of directors. Early REA borrowers tended to be small cooperatives that purchased power at wholesale rates for distribution to members. As these systems grew, however, many expanded into generating and transmission cooperatives in order to lessen their dependence on outside power sources. This trend has continued in recent years as cooperatives have not only built their own generating plants but have become extensively involved in major generating project joint ventures with investor-owned utilities. It is illustrative that in 1982, co-ops borrowed $6.4 billion for new generation facilities, compared with $1.7 billion for distribution and transmission facilities. 6/ Some 900 rural co-ops accounted for only 2.8 percent of total power generation in 1980, but this represents significant growth from 1.7 percent in 1970 and 0.7 percent in 1960. 7/

Power pools and coordination agreements: In many areas of the country, utility systems are now highly interconnected and operate under a variety of formal or informal coordination agreements. There are six "tight" power pools operating in the United States that have established arrangements for joint planning on a single system basis, centralized dispatch of system generating units and capacity reserve requirements. Four of these tight pools consist of single utility holding companies with operations in more than one state and the other two are multi-utility pools. Together, these tight interstate power pools account for about 24 percent of the nation's total generating capacity.

In addition to these tight power pools, there are eight multi-utility "loose" power pools where planning is coordinated but there are no contractual reserve requirements. Five of these loose pools operate in more than one state, and together they represent 17 percent of national generating capacity. Table 4 shows the major interstate power pools.

## The Major Participants in Electric Utility Regulation

Electric utilities are chartered by states to provide an adequate and reliable supply of electricity at reasonable prices. Each utility has been granted a monopoly franchise to construct facilities and provide power to a specified service territory. In return for this monopoly power, utilities have ceded to regulatory authorities control over entry and exit from the business, over the rates that can be charged to consumers and over the amount of profits that can be earned. This regulatory authority is exercised at two levels--the

Table 4.

## Major Interstate Power Pools

| Affected States | Name of Pool | Generating Capability Summer 1979 Megawatts |
|---|---|---|
| **Multi-State "Tight" Power Pools** | | |
| ME, VT, NH, MA, RI, CT | New England Power Pool NEPOOL | 21,294 |
| PA, NJ, MD, DE | Pennsylvania-New Jersey-Maryland Interconnection PJM | 44,891 |
| PA, WV, MD, OH, VA | Allegheny Power System Inc. APS | 6,822 |
| IN, MI, OH, WV, KY, VA, TN | American Electric Power System AEP | 20,123 |
| LA, MS, AR, MO | Middle South Utilities Inc. MSU | 12,177 |
| MS, AL, GA, FL | Southern Co. System SOCO | 23,909 |
| | Total | 129,216 |
| **Multi-State "Loose" Power Pools** | | |
| OH, PA | Central Area Power Coordination Group CAPCO | 15,147 |
| IL, MO | Illinois-Missouri Pool IL-MO | 13,480 |
| WI, IA, MN, ND, SD, NE, MT | Mid-Continent Area Power Pool MAPP | 24,527 |
| KS, MO | Missouri-Kansas Pool MOKAN | 8,879 |
| | Pacific Northwest Coordination Agreement PNCA | 32,292 |
| | Total | 94,325 |

SOURCE: National Governors' Association, "Report of the NGA Task Force on Electric Utility Regulation," January 1983.

wholesale market, or sales between utilities, and the retail level, or sales to ultimate consumers. In general, federal authorities regulate the wholesale market, and states regulate retail rates.

Federal involvement: The Federal Power Act of 1935 authorized the Federal Power Commission to license all hydroelectric projects undertaken by private utilities, order interconnections and wheeling of electric power under emergency conditions and set interstate transmission and wholesale power rates. Federal responsibility for these areas continues in force today, although with the creation of a Department of Energy in 1977 these regulatory responsibilities were split between the Federal Energy Regulatory Commission (FERC) and DOE's Economic Regulatory Administration. FERC is responsible for regulating wholesale power rates and rates on the interstate transmission of power. The Economic Regulatory Administration is responsible for enforcing the Fuel Use Act and other DOE regulations. Federal authorities also control retail electric rates in areas served by federally owned power systems.

The federal regulatory role was strengthened by Congress in 1978 through the passage of the Public Utilities Regulatory Policies Act (PURPA), which was designed to promote the conservation of electricity, cogeneration and alternative energy sources. The law required state commissions to consider a specific set of rate reforms. It also required utilities to interconnect with small power producers and to pay them for energy based on the principle of "avoided costs."

Other important areas where federal agencies are involved in utility regulation include nuclear power development (Nuclear Regulatory Commission), environmental regulations (Environmental Protection Agency), and financial practices and business transactions of holding companies (Securities and Exchange Commission).

State regulatory responsibilities: All activities of investor-owned electric utilities outside federal jurisdiction are subject to state regulation. This regulatory authority is generally assigned to a state public service or public utility commission. At present, 11 states have elected utility commissions, and the other 39 and the District of Columbia have appointed commissions. In addition to authority over retail rates, most state utility commissions have the authority to initiate financial and management audits, set company performance standards, establish automatic rate adjustment mechanisms and provide for consumer representation during regulatory proceedings. Many also have jurisdiction over such matters as accounting procedures, mergers and dispositions of property, financing arrangements, power plant and transmission line siting and utility expansion plans.

### The Debate Over Electricity's Future Role

A debate is now raging within the energy community over the role that electricity will play in the energy economy of the future. The debate involves a wide variety of participants, ranging from utility and government planners to environmentalists and consumer groups. Although the debate touches a number of complex issues, it centers on whether the shift toward electricity as the fuel of choice will continue. While differences of opinion remain about the rate of growth in overall energy demand, there is a growing consensus that overall energy demand will rise only modestly through the end of this century. Exxon and the Department of Energy, for example, agree that total U.S. energy consumption will grow at slightly less than 1 percent annually to the year 2000. 8/

But there is little agreement on the slicing of the pie--the extent to which new power plants are needed to meet demand that will arise from continued substitution of electricity for other energy sources or the implications flowing from a judgment that electricity demand will grow. Conventional wisdom says that electricity demand will continue to grow as energy consumers in all four end-use sectors-- residential, commercial, industrial and transportation--substitute electricity for increasingly expensive oil and natural gas. But an alternative point of view now argues that a greater role for electricity is unwarranted on economic grounds and will carry such heavy social costs, ranging from acid rain to nuclear plant accidents, that consumers eventually will turn away from greater use of electricity in favor of investments in energy-saving equipment and renewable energy sources. As Electrical World writes, "forecasters seem to be slowly polarizing in their analyses of load growth . . . . There are those who see the growth in electricity consumption closely correlated with the growth in the gross national product. The second camp foresees a strongly declining or even negative trend, primarily the result of conservation induced by rising prices." 9/ Perhaps no other issue will be as important to prudent energy planning in the years ahead as a correct assessment of the answer to this debate.

The case for further electrification: The majority of energy planners associated with industry and government agree that regardless of how fast the total demand for energy grows in the United States, electric power will continue to absorb an increasing share of that demand. A major energy study released by the National Academy of Sciences in 1979, for instance, states that the "many advantages of electricity for the consumer--and the motivation to substitute it where practical for uncertain oil and gas supplies--are strong reasons for believing that it will continue to grow faster than total energy use for some time into the future." 10/ Similarly, a research report published recently by the Institute for Energy Analysis found that "the virtues of electricity constitute its unique 'form value' that would lead, on strictly economic grounds, to its expanded use." 11/ Even Exxon,

Table 5.

### Percentages of Energy Consumption by Form of Energy Used, for 1982, and Projections for 2000

| Energy source | 1982 | Year 2000 | | | |
| --- | --- | --- | --- | --- | --- |
| | | EIA | OPP | DRI | RFF |
| Coal | 4.0 | 9 | 10 | 7 | 10 |
| Gas | 21.2 | 18 | 20 | 17 | 17 |
| Liquids | 40.6 | 31 | 25 | 33 | 33 |
| Electricity | 34.1 | 38 | 41 | 42 | 40 |
| Other | -- | 4 | 4 | 1 | -- |

SOURCES: Data for 1982 are from U.S. Department of Energy, Monthly Energy Review (May 1983). Projections for the year 2000 are as follows: EIA--Energy Information Administration, 1981 Annual Report to Congress, Vol. III (1982); OPP-- U.S. Department of Energy, Office of Policy, Planning and Analysis, Energy Projections to the Year 2000 (1981); DRI-- Data Resources Inc., Energy Review (1982); RFF--Resources for the Future, Energy in America's Future (1979). (Note that these energy forms apply only to end-use deliveries of energy, although they are expressed in terms of primary inputs.)

which competes in some markets with utility-supplied electric power, forecasts that electricity demand in the United States will grow at nearly three times the rate of total U.S. energy demand through the year 2000. 12/

This assessment of an increased role for electricity in the energy economy is supported by virtually all recent conventional energy studies that consider the issue of the changing mix of energy consumption. As shown in Table 5, most of these studies project that by the year 2000 primary energy consumption for electric power generation will account for about 40 percent of total energy consumption.

The case for further electrification of the economy received additional support in 1983 from a study pushed by the Reagan administration. After a two-year policy review by the Department of Energy's Office of Policy, Planning and Analysis, the Energy Department concluded the existing utility regulatory structure has held rates too low, leading to underinvestment in the industry that could result in inadequate supplies later in the decade. "Current utility plans for new electric supply do not include all the new supply that is needed to maintain reliable service through the end of the century," the DOE study found. "Unless utilities expand supply beyond current plans, supply will become inadequate to serve demand by 1997 if demand grows slowly, by 1993 if demand grows moderately, and by 1990 if demand grows fast. Indeed, since utility supply plans have persistently been revised downward and since electric supply is not distributed evenly throughout the nation, electric service in many areas may become unreliable even sooner," the study says. 13/ "We can't find anything to suggest that electricity will grow slower than the economy, so at 3 percent demand growth, half the capacity we will need in the year 2000 does not now exist," notes Steven Herod, director of the DOE research effort. 14/

In general, the electric utility industry remains a strong supporter of this thesis that electricity should play an expanded role in the country's energy future, although the industry can no longer be categorized as a monolithic supporter of anything. "We know, of course, that electricity demand will increase far more rapidly--perhaps doubling or even tripling--than overall energy use between now and the end of this century," states W. Donham Crawford, chairman and chief executive officer of Gulf States Utilities. 15/

Indeed, industry executives argue that continued development of electrical generating capacity is absolutely necessary to assure the energy supplies required for future economic growth. Without continued construction of central station generating plants, they say, the country will be caught short when the economy turns around and any long-lived economic upturn will itself be aborted by the lack of adequate power supplies. At that point, industry officials say, the United States may well face blackouts or brownouts or be forced to build uneconomic gas-fired capacity to meet new load growth. The Electric Power Research Institute (EPRI), for instance, recently completed a study which projects that 270 gigawatts of new capacity are needed by 1991 to support economic growth, provide for the retirement of aging plants, and reduce dependence on oil and gas. The EPRI study concludes that "there is not an electricity supply crisis currently but there is a planning crisis." 16/

Industry officials acknowledge that they have a credibility problem because of overly optimistic forecasting in the past, but they say that, if anything, this phenomenon has now caused industry forecasters to react too far in the other direction. As Chauncey Starr, vice chairman of EPRI, puts it, "The utility industry went through a long optimistic period when growth was 'in' and utility planning for future requirements inevitably crowded the upper edge of the demand uncertainty band. We are now in a pessimistic period when growth is a burden. To the extent that utilities, regulatory commissions, and government agencies acknowledge potential growth officially, they are obligated to do something about it. Consequently, growth projections now crowd the lower edge of the uncertainty band of demand." 17/

In addition to this theory that forecasts are always biased in favor of current conditions, utility industry officials and others who foresee increased reliance on electricity tend to base their case on one or more of the following assumptions:

-- Increased use of electricity is the only way to utilize those resources that are most abundant domestically--coal and uranium--and reduce the country's dependence on imported oil.

-- Electricity will be required for U.S. economic growth in general and specifically for many of the emerging industries such as computers and robotics that are vital to a recovery of U.S. industrial productivity and growth.

-- Electricity prices will rise considerably more slowly than the prices of competing fuels--particularly oil and natural gas.

This last assumption appears particularly crucial to the case for continued market penetration by electricity and vigorous demand growth, since much of the gains in market share by electricity over the last two decades have been attributed to its falling price relative to other fuels. Nearly all forecasters who foresee a growing role for electricity expect the relative price of electric power to fall. The assumption behind the DOE study, for instance, is that electricity prices will rise only one-third as fast as other energy prices. 18/ Similarly, ICF Incorporated, a Washington consulting firm that does consulting work for utilities and the Department of Energy, says its studies indicate that "absent major shocks in energy markets, electric rates will increase at a slower rate during the 1980s than during the 1970s, reducing the rate of growth in conservation efforts." 19/ John Siegel of the Atomic Industrial Forum and John Sillin of Booz, Allen & Hamilton recently made the case for a similar scenario in a journal article that concluded:

> Real electricity prices will not head up, but will stabilize or decline over the next 10 years....In addition, the price gains achieved by electricity relative to oil and natural gas should be maintained. As a result, electricity will continue to gain a growing share of the total energy market--and this growth may be enhanced by technological advances which increase or improve on the applications to which electricity can be put. This growth in market share, when combined with economic recovery, may result in electric load growth rates which will exceed those currently being projected by utility and nonutility forecasters alike. 20/

The case against further electrification: While most energy analysts predict a continuation of past trends toward greater use of electricity in end-use applications relative to other forms of energy, in recent years an alternative school of thought that holds that further electrification would be uneconomic, inefficient and perhaps socially undesirable has challenged this reasoning. These analysts argue that the United States already has enough electrical capacity to meet those needs for which electric power is best suited--such as lighting and electric motors--indefinitely. Using electricity for tasks such as space and water heating is inherently inefficient, these analysts say, and can only increase the amount of energy being wasted in the conversion process.

The case against greater electrification of the economy was first made in a comprehensive fashion in 1975 by physicist Amory Lovins, who presented it as part of his opposition to continued development of nuclear power. Lovins argued that "two main policy paths for the rich countries are now rapidly diverging, and we must jump for one or the other. The first is high-energy, nuclear, centralized, electric; the second is lower energy, fission-free, decentralized, less electrified, softer-technology based on energy income." According to Lovins, economic, technical and social constraints led one "irresistibly to conclude that the comparatively simple, low-technology, decentralized, non-electrical energy technologies make the most sense." 21/

Lovins's arguments quickly found support among analysts associated with the environmental and antinuclear movements; his economic case dovetailed nicely with their long-held beliefs that nuclear and coal-fired generating plants were a menace to the environment. More recently, however, Lovins's ideas about renewable energy sources--expanded to include many least-cost energy efficiency improvements--have also attracted considerable support from independent economists, Wall Street utility analysts and even a few utilities. While many energy analysts disagree with various aspects of Lovins's "soft path" approach, a considerable number of them have adopted Lovins's conclusions on the specific question of the economic role for electricity. Roger W. Sant, for instance, director of the Energy Productivity Center of the Mellon Institute and former deputy director of the Federal Energy Administration, has argued in a study called The Least-Cost Energy Strategy that utility-supplied electric power generation is too expensive to compete in today's energy market and that the most significant energy investments in the next decade will be in products that improve energy efficiency. According to the Sant study, if the only objective had been to provide people with the energy services they wanted in 1978 at the lowest possible cost, centrally generated electricity should have provided only 17 percent of total energy demand (in terms of primary inputs) rather than the 30 percent it did. "At current costs, most new central power generation is too expensive to compete in the energy services marketplace," Sant wrote in 1981. "Electric utilities are experiencing this problem now--and it should become more evident in the early part of this decade," he adds. 22/ Lovins agrees, arguing in a recent essay that "debating which new power stations to build is like shopping for the best buy in brandy to burn in your car or for Chippendales to burn in your stove. Regardless of what kind of new power station yields the cheapest electricity," Lovins says, "no kind can nearly compete with the real competitors--the cheapest ways to provide the same energy services, such as comfort. These include weatherstripping, insulation, greenhouses, heat exchangers, and window-shading and -insulating devices." 23/

Similarly, a major study published in 1981 by the federally funded Solar Energy Research Institute found that if consumers choose to make cost-effective investments in energy-saving equipment, electric utilities, on a national basis, will have too much capacity through the end of the century unless all of the following occur: (1) use of electric trains and electric cars expands greatly; (2) no new generating capacity is brought on line after 1985; (3) all fossil fuel plants built before 1961 are retired; (4) 80 percent of all oil- and gas-fired capacity is retired; (5) capacity factors are not improved through better load management; and (6) no cogeneration or solar electric capacity is added. 24/

Finally, the Congressional Research Service recently weighed in on the side of those who believe that talk of electricity supply shortages is premature. After examining electric power supply and demand forecasts on a national and regional basis, Alvin Kaufman, CRS's senior specialist in regulatory economics, has concluded that "there do not appear to be any electricity supply-demand problems by 1990" and that minor problems could occur by 1995 only "if no weight is given to the contribution of 'least cost' methods." 25/ In fact, Kaufman argues that federal policies have been so overly generous to utility expansion that "given the emerging realization that the industry may well be overbuilt, and may remain that way for some years to come, it may be necessary to reexamine federal policies toward utilities and to consider alternative strategies for the industry." 26/

For many analysts, the dramatic increases in electricity rates in recent years are a key factor in projecting stagnant electricity demand growth. According to George McNamee, president of the regional brokerage and investment firm First Albany Corp., "the evidence has shown that the demand for electricity is price elastic--as prices rise, demand falls." In McNamee's view, "by the time some of these new [generating] plants are built the demand won't be there" to allow the utilities to recover their investments. 27/ Even Electrical World, an industry trade publication that continues to predict strong electricity demand growth, acknowledges that the case for little further demand growth is becoming stronger. "Adding to the rate base the roughly 60 gw (gigawatts) of nuclear plants to be completed over the next 10 years will effect drastic jumps in rates for the systems involved," Electrical World notes. "If, in addition to the rising cost of electric energy, you postulate that all other forms of energy will be in a relative surplus during the next decade, electricity may also lose some of its advantage during that period, further depressing its use," the trade journal says. 28/

Overall, analysts who believe that utility-generated electricity has saturated its major markets and that electricity use will grow very slowly, if at all, between now and the year 2000 base their case on one or more of the following assumptions:

-- Total energy demand will remain steady or fall over the next 20 years as consumers continue to invest in energy-saving processes and equipment.

-- The market for utility-generated electric power will face greatly increased competition from decentralized generating technologies that will be owned and operated by electricity consumers.

-- Electricity prices will rise at a faster pace than the prices of competing fuels, particularly coal and various renewable energy sources.

The debate over the role electricity will play in the nation's energy future is not likely to be resolved soon. The issues involved are complex and the stakes are enormous. Moreover, the actions advocated by each side are diametrically opposed and in many cases may be mutually exclusive. As Edward P. Larkin, president of the National Association of Regulatory Commissioners, puts it, "The industry is between a rock and a hard place. If they overbuild they will be penalized. If they underbuild they will be penalized even more." 29/

## CHAPTER II FOOTNOTES

1.  Arthur A. Thompson, "The Strategic Dilemma of Electric Utilities--Part I," Public Utilities Fortnightly, March 18, 1982, p. 20.

2.  Energy Information Administration, Monthly Energy Review, September 1983, p. 24.

3.  Edison Electric Institute, "1982 Annual Electric Power Survey," April 1983; also "34th Annual Electric Utility Industry Forecast," Electrical World, September 1983, p. 59.

4.  Michael Bergman, "Electric Utility Statistics, 1882-1982," Public Power, September-October 1982, pp. 65-67.

5.  Mary C. Going, "Annual Statistical Report," Electrical World, March 1983, p. 75.

6.  Ibid., p. 84.

7.  Bergman, op. cit.

8.  Exxon Corp., World Energy Outlook, December 1980, p. 30; and Energy Information Administration, 1981 Annual Report to Congress, Vol. 3, February 1982, p. 176.

9.  "Recession Causes Industry's First Decline in Peak," Electrical World, September 1982, p. 83.

10. National Academy of Sciences, "U.S. Energy Supply Prospects to 2010," The Report of the Supply and Delivery Panel to the Committee on Nuclear and Alternative Energy Systems (Washington, D.C., National Academy of Sciences, 1979), p. 34.

11. "Will Electricity Continue Gains in Energy Use?," Electrical World, May 1982, p. 26.

12. Exxon Corp., op. cit., p. 12.

13. U.S. Department of Energy, The Future of Electric Power in America: Economic Supply for Economic Growth, Office of Policy, Planning and Analysis, June 1983, p. 4-5.

14. J. Steven Herod, presentation at Government Institutes "Electricity Regulation Seminar," Washington, D.C., March 2, 1983.

15. W. Donham Crawford, "The Electric Utility Executives Forum," Public Utilities Fortnightly, April 9, 1981, p. 78.

16. Electric Power Research Institute, "Generating Capacity in U.S. Electric Utilities," EPRI EA-2639-SR, October 1982, p. 4-1.

17. Chauncey Starr, "Letter to the Editor," Harvard Business Review, September-October 1982, p. 176.

18. See J. Steven Herod and Jeffrey Skeer, "The Nation's Electric Future: Perspectives on Electricity Supply Sufficiency," in Diversification, Deregulation, and Increased Uncertainty in the Public Utility Industries (East Lansing, Michigan State University, 1983), p. 253.

19. Robert Spann and Steven Wade, "The Decline and Fall of Electric Utility Growth Rates," March 1983, p. 35.

20. John R. Siegel and John O. Sillin, "Changes in the Real Price of Electricity: Implications for Higher Load Growth," Public Utilities Fortnightly, September 15, 1983, p. 42.

21. Amory B. Lovins, Non-Nuclear Futures: The Case for an Ethical Energy Strategy (London, Friends of the Earth, 1975), p. xxvi.

22. Roger W. Sant, "The Economics of Energy and the Environment," The Energy Consumer, January 1981, p. 12.

23. Amory B. Lovins and L. Hunter Lovins, "Electric Utilities: Key to Capitalizing the Energy Transition," Technological Forecasting and Social Change, 22-1982, p. 158.

24. Solar Energy Research Institute, A New Prosperity--The SERI Solar/Conservation Study (Andover, Mass., Brick House Publishing, 1981), p. 328.

25. Alvin Kaufman and Karen Nelson, "An Assessment of the Need for New Electric Capacity," Congressional Research Service, Report No. 83-558 S, August 31, 1983, p. ix.

26. Alvin Kaufman and Karen Nelson, "Do We Really Need All Those Electric Plants," Congressional Research Service, August 1982, p. 17.

27. Michael Clowes, "First Albany Even Bests Wall Street--Sometimes," Pensions and Investment Age, May 1980.

28. "Recession Causes Industry's First Decline in Peak," op. cit., p. 83.

29. Edward P. Larkin, speech at the Edison Electric Institute Seminar on Utility Finances, New York, N.Y., Oct. 27, 1981.

# III
# PRESSURES
# ON THE
# ELECTRIC UTILITY INDUSTRY

Portions of the electric utility industry are in serious trouble. The industry has financial problems that rank its weakest members among the least creditworthy of major U.S. companies. But perhaps even more important, it faces conflicting social and economic pressures that are intense and growing. Many electric utilities are confronting a need for substantial rate increases over the next several years; growing public opposition to those increases; a staggering need for external capital; a loss of credibility among segments of the public and the regulatory community; heightened concern and scrutiny from investors and financial institutions; stagnant sales growth; and greatly increased competition from decentralized electric power sources, publicly owned utilities and other forms of energy. In the words of Frank W. Griffith, chairman of the Edison Electric Institute, "The electric utility business is no longer the neatly arranged, tidy, well-organized operation we once experienced. It is changing from day to day, profoundly influenced by events beyond our borders and most assuredly beyond our control. We are attacked on every front, sometimes even by those whom we had counted as friends." [1]

The pressures on electric utilities are not really new; they date back more than a decade now. What is new is a growing perception by industry observers and utility managements that some of the problems the industry faces are not temporary ones attributable to transitory economic phenomena--the high inflation of the 1970s or the high interest rates of the last several years. Rather, the industry's problems are coming to be seen as more permanent in nature and stemming from fundamental structural changes, both economic and social, that have taken place in the industry's business environment--problems that will require consideration of new regulatory and management alternatives as electric utilities plan for the future.

Early development--an orientation toward growth: For most of the electric utility industry's history, a consensus has existed within the industry that the proper basic business strategy for a utility was based on the promotion of electricity sales and the construction of new central-station power plants to meet that demand. This "grow and build" strategy, as it has been called, became the predominant force guiding the industry's planning.

There are a number of reasons for the industry's historical orientation toward growth through expanding electricity sales and building more power plants. First, it is important to note that a decision was made early in the industry's history that electric utilities would sell electric current as their principal product rather than the energy services such as heating and lighting that people were actually interested in. As Roger Sant has described it, in 1898, about 20 years after Thomas Edison invented the incandescent light bulb, New York Edison--the country's first electric utility--began selling electricity in kilowatt-hours rather than light-hours. The change marked a shift away from the sale of end-use energy services to the sale of electric energy itself--a change that Thomas Edison strongly opposed. From that point on, electric utilities focused primarily on increasing their sales of electric power regardless of the developments taking place in the products that used electricity. As Edison himself noted in 1898, this led to an inherent contradiction between the goals of electric utilities and those of consumers:

> Another reason I did not want to sell current was that from my experiments, I knew that the incandescent lamp was only the beginning and that there were great possibilities of enormously increasing its economy . . . .

> But for some reason . . . the selling of current was introduced, thus destroying all chances of the company's gaining any benefits in [lamp] improvements; in fact, such improvements were a disadvantage, which in my mind is a poor business policy for the company and for the public. 2/

In addition to this early business decision that oriented the industry toward an emphasis on electric power sales, the grow and build strategy was supported until recently by the economics of new power plant construction, the structure of the industry's regulatory system, and the nature of the industry's obligation to serve the public.

Throughout most of this century, declining marginal costs in the industry acted as a strong incentive to build new power plants. During this period, a continuing series of inventions and innovations in the electric power field led to declining generating and distribution costs and rapid growth in per capita electricity usage. This growth fed upon itself as economies of scale and improvements in plant steam conditions, metallurgy, and operating temperatures pushed electric companies to build ever larger and more efficient fossil-fueled generating units and as the country's abundant hydroelectric resources were tapped for power generation. Fossil fuel supplies were readily available and, during the 1950s and 1960s, their prices declined steadily in real terms. Large hydroelectric plants produced low-cost power and were virtually inflation-proof because the fuel --water--was free and operating costs were low. Industry regulators served chiefly to allocate the benefits of declining costs between utility stockholders and ratepayers as companies went through a predictable cycle of increased demand, greater efficiency, lower costs, higher profits and lower rates. Economies of scale dictated that each new power plant be larger than the last. Meanwhile, regulatory lags--the designated nemesis of today's electric utility executive--served to fatten company profit margins by preventing lower costs from being passed on immediately to consumers through lower rates. In the words of Arthur Thompson, an economist at the University of Alabama:

> Prior to the late 1960s, the electric utility business was such that companies could build new generating plants, extend their transmission and distribution networks, improve the reliability of service, meet the growing needs of customers for electricity, and still be in position to charge a lower average price per kilowatt-hour . . . . It was truly a golden age in which to be in the electric utility business. 3/

Utility growth was further motivated by the way utilities are allowed a rate of return on their rate base. This rate base generally consists of all fixed plant and equipment in use to provide service to customers. Consequently, if a utility was already earning its allowed profit margin, the only way it could increase profits was to build new power plants and distribution systems. Meanwhile, federal tax breaks favored the most capital-intensive technologies, such as nuclear power. As a major study by the Solar Energy Research Institute summed up the situation: "Existing regulation often has the effect of discouraging investments in energy efficiency and of providing so much protection for large utility plants, which involve large financial risks in times of demand uncertainty, that market signals that would discourage such investments are not able to work effectively." 4/

Finally, the utility industry was encouraged to grow and build by the nature of its obligation to serve the needs of the public. As part of the contract by which electric utilities are granted territorial monopolies over power supplies and distribution, they are obligated to maintain sufficient generating capacity to meet all anticipated customer demand. Utilities and regulators have generally interpreted this requirement as an absolute, irrespective of the trade-offs between reliability of service and price. Also, because demand forecasting is an inherently uncertain process, utilities traditionally chose to be conservative in their forecasts and err on the side of over-building rather than risk being caught short of generating capacity by an unexpected uptick in electricity demand growth.

An industry transformed: All of this changed in the early 1970s when, in a few short years, a number of factors converged to reverse the industry's decreasing marginal cost character. In general, these forces can be divided into two major types, although because they are interrelated it is often difficult to distinguish between them. First, the industry was confronted with financial pressures resulting from changes in underlying economic and technological conditions that had a particularly dramatic impact on electric utilities--rising fuel costs, persistent inflation and high interest rates, a slowdown in economic growth and technological innovation, and increased competition. At the same time, however, the industry was faced with financial and strategic pressures arising from greater regulation and the increasing politicization of the utility decisionmaking process. Together, these forces transformed the entire economic structure of the industry, although the changes were almost imperceptible at first. Some of the pressures on electric utilities--such as rising fuel costs and inflation--have eased substantially as the industry entered the 1980s. Other pressures, however, such as increased competition and the politicization of utility planning, are becoming more acute.

## Pressures from Economic Conditions

Fuel cost increases: As it entered the decade of the 1970s, the electric utility industry was extremely dependent on fossil fuels for its generating plants. In 1970, for instance, coal, petroleum and natural gas consumption accounted for 82 percent of the industry's total electric power production--with coal providing about 56 percent of this total. 5/ Thus, the industry was very heavily exposed to the increases in fossil fuel prices that began in the late 1960s, accelerated in the early 1970s and still continue. In constant dollar terms, the price of coal hit a low in 1968. It has more than tripled since that time. 6/ Similarly, constant-dollar crude oil and natural gas prices, after declining for more than a decade, hit lows in 1970 and 1972, respectively, and began rising dramatically after the 1973 Arab oil embargo. 7/ As shown in Table 6, the weighted average cost (in current dollars) of all fossil fuels delivered to electric utilities has jumped nearly five-fold since 1973, from 47.5 to 222.5 cents per million Btu. One industry analyst recently calculated that fuel price increases since 1970 increased the industry's fuel costs by $30.2 billion in 1980 alone--almost eight times the industry's total fuel bill a decade earlier. 8/

Even utilities that have pursued nuclear power development have been unable to escape escalating fuel costs completely. The spot market price of uranium oxide rose from about $6 a pound in 1972 to $45 a pound in 1979, although it has recently fallen back to around $22 a pound as utilities have canceled nuclear units and attempted to sell off unneeded uranium inventories. Meanwhile, government uranium enrichment fees have been rising sharply as a result of reduced

Table 6.

### Average Cost of Fossil Fuels Delivered
### to Steam-Electric Utility Plants, 1973-82
(current dollars)

| Year | Coal | Residual Oil | Natural Gas | All Fossil Fuels |
|------|------|------|------|------|
| | | (cents per million Btu) | | |
| 1973 | 40.5 | 78.8 | 33.8 | 47.5 |
| 1974 | 71.0 | 191.0 | 48.1 | 90.9 |
| 1975 | 81.4 | 201.4 | 75.4 | 103.0 |
| 1976 | 84.8 | 195.9 | 103.4 | 110.4 |
| 1977 | 94.7 | 220.4 | 130.0 | 127.7 |
| 1978 | 111.6 | 212.3 | 143.8 | 139.3 |
| 1979 | 122.4 | 299.7 | 175.4 | 162.1 |
| 1980 | 135.1 | 427.9 | 221.4 | 190.4 |
| 1981 | 153.2 | 529.4 | 282.5 | 222.5 |
| 1982 | 164.7 | 475.5 | 340.6 | 222.5 |

SOURCE:  Energy Information Administration, Monthly Energy Review, June 1983.

projections of future enrichment demand and the increased cost of electric power to operate the government's gaseous diffusion enrichment plants.  Energy Department fixed-commitment enrichment contracts now cost about $135 per separative work unit (SWU) compared with $35 per SWU in 1974. 9/

Skyrocketing fuel costs have adversely affected electric utilities in several ways.  First, although public utility commissions have granted most utilities the ability to pass through increases in their fuel costs directly to customers through "fuel adjustment clauses," lags between the time the added costs are incurred and the revenues are recovered have weakened utilities' cash flows.  In addition, because these added costs have directly affected customers they have been a strong factor in motivating customers' conservation efforts.  Finally, the highly visible nature of price increases related to utility fuel adjustment clauses has made them a lightning rod for consumer and regulatory actions against utilities.  Recently, some utilities have had automatic fuel adjustment clauses suspended by public utility commissions in response to investigations into their fuel procurement practices, while in other states political pressures are mounting for abolition of fuel adjustment clauses altogether.  Missouri and Michigan have already prohibited use of utility fuel adjustment clauses, and a recent survey indicated that legislation is currently pending in 15 additional states that would prohibit or restrict such use. 10/ Overall, although residual oil prices have recently fallen somewhat, coal and natural gas prices have continued to rise, and most analysts expect that rising fuel costs will continue to present major problems for the industry in coming decades.

High inflation and interest rates: The increasing rate of inflation and accompanying higher interest rates that characterized the 1970s were another source of tremendous cost pressure on the utility industry because they came at a time when the industry was anticipating rapid growth and was heavily committed to a capital-intensive construction schedule. From 1965-70, the annual inflation rate as measured by the Commerce Department's fixed-weighted price index averaged 4.0 percent. For the period 1970-75 this average rose to 6.6 percent, and for 1975-80 it rose to 7.8 percent. Similarly, Table 7 shows that the average interest rate on new long-term debt issued by the industry increased dramatically during the 1970s and early 1980s, causing a steady rise in the embedded interest rate on the industry's long-term debt.

Higher inflation and interest rates affected all businesses during the 1970s, of course, but electric utilities were particularly vulnerable to these economic forces for a number of reasons--the extremely capital-intensive nature of the industry; the higher-than-average rates of inflation experienced by goods and services needed by the industry; and regulation, which often prevented increased costs from being immediately passed on to consumers. Overall, high inflation and interest rates during the 1970s adversely affected electric utilities in a number of areas, with the most important being higher construction, operation and maintenance, and financing costs.

Construction costs--If any category of utility costs has risen faster than the cost of fossil fuels in the last 15 years, it is the cost of constructing new electric generating capacity. According to the Department of Energy, the average installed cost per kilowatt of capacity of new generating plants in excess of 300 megawatts was generally falling during the years before 1967, despite inflation in the general economy. 11/ This had the effect of encouraging utilities to build ever larger, more complex plants in hopes of attaining ever greater levels of efficiency. Beginning in 1967, however, and continuing through the present, the average cost of new generating capacity has increased at a rate substantially in excess of the general inflation rate. The average cost of newly installed generating capacity rose from $140 per kilowatt during the period 1960-69 to $531 per kilowatt during 1970-79, and is projected to rise to at least $1,300/kw during the 1980s. 12/

All types of utility generating plants have experienced rapid cost escalation, but experts agree that nuclear plant capital costs have risen the fastest. In a book entitled Power Plant Cost Escalation that is the most comprehensive study of the subject to date, energy con-

Table 7.

### Interest Rates on Utility Debt, 1965-82

| Year | Long-Term Debt Average Embedded Interest Rate | Average Interest Rate on New Long-Term Debt |
|------|-----------------------------------------------|---------------------------------------------|
| 1965 | 3.8% | 4.6% |
| 1966 | 3.9 | 5.5 |
| 1967 | 4.1 | 6.1 |
| 1968 | 4.3 | 6.8 |
| 1969 | 4.6 | 8.0 |
| 1970 | 5.1 | 8.8 |
| 1971 | 5.5 | 7.7 |
| 1972 | 5.7 | 7.5 |
| 1973 | 6.0 | 7.9 |
| 1974 | 6.5 | 9.6 |
| 1975 | 6.9 | 10.0 |
| 1976 | 7.1 | 8.9 |
| 1977 | 7.3 | 8.4 |
| 1978 | 7.5 | 9.3 |
| 1979 | 7.8 | 10.9 |
| 1980 | 8.4 | 13.5 |
| 1981 | 9.3 | 16.4 |
| 1982P | 9.6 | 15.1 |

P = Preliminary

SOURCE:    Edison Electric Institute.

sultant Charles Komanoff found that between 1971 and 1978, nuclear plant capital costs increased at a rate of 13.5 percent annually <u>above</u> the general rate of inflation in the construction sector, with much of the increase due to tighter regulatory standards that caused expensive design and construction changes on plants already under construction. 13/  For coal plants, Komanoff found that capital costs increased 7.7 percent annually in excess of construction sector inflation, with about half of the total increase due to the addition of stack gas scrubbing equipment. In both of these estimates, Komanoff excludes the effect of added financing costs. Thus, the trend toward building large nuclear power plants that occurred in the 1970s and continues today has been a particularly important factor in rising utility construction expenditures.

The astonishing increases that have occurred in generating plant, and especially nuclear plant, construction costs are perhaps best illustrated by comparing the costs of two mid-Atlantic nuclear plants. In 1967, the Haddam Neck nuclear unit in Connecticut became the first commercial-size (more than 500 megawatts) nuclear reactor to generate electricity for the utility industry. The unit had an installed capacity cost of $195/kw. 14/ In the same year that the Haddam Neck unit went on line, Long Island Lighting ordered the Shoreham nuclear plant. After suffering a number of delays and construction changes, the Shoreham plant is now scheduled to begin commercial operation in 1985 at a cost of about $4,200/kw. Moreover, Long Island Lighting warns that its most recent cost estimate is now low and that recent problems with the unit's diesel generators will lead to additional delays, adding $40-45/kw for every month of delay. The findings of a blue ribbon panel appointed by New York Gov. Mario Cuomo suggest that the plant will ultimately cost more than $5000/kw. 15/

The Shoreham unit is admittedly something of an extreme example of an expensive generating unit, but it is by no means an isolated case. The rate of cost escalation for nuclear units appears, if anything, to have increased since the completion of Komanoff's study, and it now looks as if there are at least a dozen half-built nuclear units that will cost more than $4,000/kw to construct if these units are not canceled. 16/

The significance of these increases in construction costs for the deterioration in financial condition that the electric utility industry has experienced is heightened by the sheer magnitude of the industry's construction program. According to the U.S. Commerce Department's Bureau of Economic Analysis, the electric utility industry has accounted for about 10 percent of total private non-farm capital investment in the United States in recent years. 17/ The bulk of this spending has been going toward nuclear and coal plant construction. 18/ While consuming about 10 percent of the nation's private investment capital, however--or more than the capital expenditures of the automotive, paper and chemical industries combined--electric utilities account for only about 2 percent of private non-farm GNP. Moreover, the 10 percent figure is somewhat understated because it excludes the burgeoning capital spending by publicly owned utilities.

The Edison Electric Institute projects that for the five-year period 1983-87, outlays for electric utility generating plant and equipment by investor-owned utilities will total $158.6 billion, a 10 percent increase from expenditures during the previous five-year period, 1978-82. 19/ About 39 percent of this total is earmarked for nuclear facilities. This compares with a total net investment in electric utility plant and equipment of about $227.3 billion as of 1981 by the investor-owned segment of the industry. 20/

If such aggregate figures of the utility industry's construction effort defy comprehension, there is another way to look at the extremely capital-intensive nature of the industry--fixed asset investment to sales ratios. As of 1980, investor-owned electric utilities had invested an average of $3.07 in utility plant to support each $1 in annual revenue from kilowatt-hour sales. 21/ In contrast, in

Figure 2.

### Utility Capital Expenditures
### Compared with Total Industrial Expenditures in 1980
(billions of dollars)

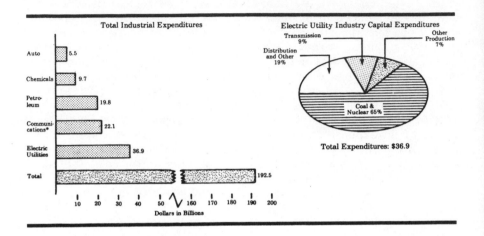

SOURCE:  U.S. Department of Energy, Energy Information Administration.

1980 General Motors had a fixed asset investment of 16 cents per dollar of sales revenue and Exxon had an investment in plant, property and equipment of 31 cents per dollar of sales revenue. 22/

A number of signs indicate that the construction spending binge that electric utilities embarked upon in the 1970s is easing. With the exception of 1980, annual electric utility capital appropriations--that is, authorizations to spend money in the future--have been falling since 1975. 23/ Meanwhile, the number of cancellations of major generating units has remained at a very high level in recent years. Since 1977, for instance, 63 nuclear units representing 70,971 megawatts of capacity have been canceled and another 13 units have been deferred indefinitely. In addition, 68 major fossil fuel units, representing 69,155 megawatts of capacity, have been canceled since 1977. 24/

But while utility capital spending budgets seem destined to fall eventually, it appears unlikely that this will result in significant relief for the industry as a whole until at least the late 1980s. Because of long construction lead times and continuing cost increases at plants under construction, actual electric utility industry capital expenditures--as distinguished from appropriations--set another new

Table 8.

### Total Electric Power System Capital Expenditures
### 1972-1982
(millions of current dollars)

| Year | Investor-owned | Total Industry |
|------|------|------|
| 1972 | 13,435 | 16,651 |
| 1973 | 14,979 | 18,723 |
| 1974 | 16,421 | 20,556 |
| 1975 | 15,130 | 20,155 |
| 1976 | 17,027 | 25,189 |
| 1977 | 19,806 | 27,711 |
| 1978 | 22,431 | 30,250 |
| 1979 | 24,445 | 35,254 |
| 1980 | 25,816 | 35,925 |
| 1981 | 27,254 | 35,823 |
| 1982 | 31,161 | 40,216 |

SOURCE:   Electrical World surveys.

annual record in 1982, reaching $40.2 billion. 25/ Capital spending trends for the investor-owned segment of the industry are illustrated in Table 8.

Capital spending at many utilities is already declining. Nevertheless, it remains clear that many utilities continue to underestimate the extent of the cost overruns they face on generating plants under construction--especially nuclear units. In 1983, for example, Public Service Co. of New Hampshire, Cincinnati Gas & Electric, Cleveland Electric, Public Service Co. of Indiana and the Tennessee Valley Authority all announced unanticipated multi-billion dollar increases in cost estimates for completing nuclear plants under construction. The common wisdom in the utility industry that most of the nuclear plant cancellations and cost increases are now past appears to be highly questionable. Perhaps the most that can be said is that capital spending patterns in the industry will vary widely depending upon individual utilities' situations and corporate strategies.

Operation and maintenance costs--Still another area of utility costs hit hard by inflation is operation and maintenance, or O&M, costs. This category includes labor, maintenance supplies and materials, administration expenses, chemicals, lubricants and water. Utility O&M costs per unit of capacity fell slightly during the 1960s but rose sharply during the 1970s, in part because of increasingly stringent environmental and safety regulations. Average (size-weighted) O&M costs for fossil-fuel steam electric plants more than tripled from 0.83 mills per kilowatt hour in 1970 to 2.98 mills/kwh in 1980. 26/ Increases in nuclear plant O&M costs have been even more pronounced, rising from 2.67 mills/kwh to 5.98 mills/kwh between 1977 and 1980 alone. 27/ Overall, O&M costs for investor-owned utilities reached $24.7 billion in 1982, a 14.1 percent jump over 1981. 28/ It is estimated that the increases in utility O&M costs during the 1970s that resulted from inflation are now adding almost $8 billion annually in extra costs to utility bills. While this represents only about one-quarter of the inflationary impact of higher fuel costs on the industry during this period, it is nonetheless very significant. Moreover, the factors contributing to increases in utility O&M costs do not appear to be leveling off. Some, in fact, are just beginning to be felt. Regulations mandating stack-gas scrubbers on new coal plants, possible retrofitting of scrubbers on older coal plants in response to concerns about acid rain, a growing shortage of power engineers in the United States and a host of new safety regulations for nuclear plants, for example, seem destined to push up average utility O&M costs at a rate well in excess of the general inflation rate for some time to come.

Financing costs--A final consequence of the chronic inflation of the 1970s was an enormous leap in utility financing costs. As Figure 3 illustrates, the cost of new utility capital has generally fluctuated in response to the underlying rate of inflation and has risen dramatically in recent years. The higher yields on utility stocks and bonds reflected in Figure 3, combined with sharp increases in the industry's outstanding long-term debt, have had a major impact on the utility industry's financing costs. Long-term debt for the investor-owned segment of the electric utility industry grew from $42.2 billion in 1970 to $124.8 billion in 1982, resulting in interest charges of about $11.5 billion in 1982. 29/ Moreover, the prospects for a quick reversal of this trend are not good, despite the dramatic drop in the rate of inflation in 1982 and 1983. Interest rates on new utility debt have dropped somewhat from their 1981 highs, but remain far above the industry's embedded cost of capital. The resulting financial attrition "can be expected to continue for some time to come," says Walter French, a utility analyst with Argus Research Corp., and "without the timely implementation of offset rate increases to recover the increased capital costs, the higher charges will cause erosion in return on common equity." 30/

Lagging technological innovation: Another contributor to higher utility costs in the last two decades has been a marked slowdown in technological innovation affecting overall power plant efficiency. The amount of fuel required to produce 1 kilowatt hour of electricity decreased with consistent regularity between the initial appearance of the steam-turbine generator around 1900 and the mid-1960s. Early coal-fired turbine generators required approximately 6 pounds of coal to produce 1 kwh of electric power. Today, the most efficient

Figure 3.

### Comparison of Earnings Yields, Aa Bond Rates and Inflation
### 1964-78

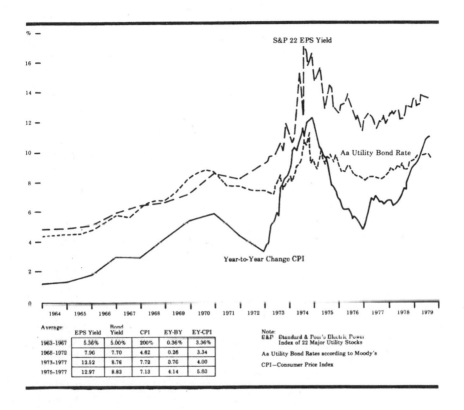

| Average: | EPS Yield | Bond Yield | CPI | EY-BY | EY-CPI |
|---|---|---|---|---|---|
| 1963-1967 | 5.36% | 5.00% | 2.00% | 0.36% | 3.36% |
| 1968-1972 | 7.96 | 7.70 | 4.62 | 0.26 | 3.34 |
| 1973-1977 | 12.52 | 8.76 | 7.72 | 3.76 | 4.80 |
| 1975-1977 | 12.97 | 8.83 | 7.13 | 4.14 | 5.83 |

Note:
S&P   Standard & Poor's Electric Power
        Index of 22 Major Utility Stocks

Aa Utility Bond Rates according to Moody's

CPI—Consumer Price Index

SOURCE: Goldman Sachs Investment Research, "Public Utility Survey--An Analytical Service."

fossil-fueled units require only seven-tenths of a pound of coal to produce 1 kwh--an 850 percent increase in thermal efficiency. 31/

Since 1966, however, there has been virtually no increase in the average thermal efficiency of utility central-station power plants. As shown in Table 9, the national average heat rate for fossil-fueled steam-electric plants has hovered near 10,400 Btus per net kwh since the mid-1960s, yielding a thermal efficiency of about 32.8 percent. Nuclear plants have also failed to achieve any significant gains in thermal efficiency and, on average, are slightly less efficient than fossil-fueled plants. As Darrell Smith, a utility consultant with

Table 9.

## National Average Heat Rates
## for Fossil-Fueled Steam-Electric Plants
### 1938, 1948, and 1958-80

| Year | Heat Rate (Btu per net kilowatt hour) | Thermal Efficiency* (percent) |
|------|----------------------------------------|-------------------------------|
| 1938 | 16,500 | 20.7 |
| 1948 | 15,738 | 21.7 |
| 1958 | 11,085 | 30.8 |
| 1959 | 10,970 | 31.1 |
| 1960 | 10,760 | 31.7 |
| 1961 | 10,650 | 32.1 |
| 1962 | 10,558 | 32.3 |
| 1963 | 10,482 | 32.6 |
| 1964 | 10,462 | 32.6 |
| 1965 | 10,453 | 32.7 |
| 1966 | 10,415 | 32.8 |
| 1967 | 10,432 | 32.7 |
| 1968 | 10,398 | 32.8 |
| 1969 | 10,447 | 32.7 |
| 1970 | 10,494 | 32.5 |
| 1971 | 10,478 | 32.6 |
| 1972 | 10,379 | 32.9 |
| 1973 | 10,389 | 32.9 |
| 1974 | 10,442 | 32.7 |
| 1975 | 10,406 | 32.8 |
| 1976 | 10,373 | 32.9 |
| 1977 | 10,435 | 32.7 |
| 1978 | 10,361 | 32.9 |
| 1979 | 10,353 | 32.9 |
| 1980 | 10,388 | 32.8 |

* Based on 3,412 Btu as the energy equivalent of 1 kwh

Note: This table includes internal combustion plants before 1958. These plants generated less than 1 percent of the total kilowatt hour output in the reported years.

---

SOURCE: FPC 1 and FPC 1M as reported by Energy Information Administration in "Thermal Electric Plant Construction Cost and Annual Production Expenses--1980," June 1983.

Temple, Barker & Sloane, puts it, "the handwriting has been on the wall for a long time that the technology being employed by the electric utility industry is maturing." 32/

The present dearth of improvement in average power plant thermal efficiency is likely to continue until the industry begins to use new technologies to generate power. Although the large new fossil-fueled units now being brought on line are, in general, somewhat more efficient than the older units that are being retired, this improvement is largely being offset by the efficiency penalties associated with advanced pollution control systems. The use of stack-gas scrubbers, cooling towers, and clean but low quality coal are all factors that reduce power plant efficiency. The next significant improvement in central station power plant thermal efficiency is not likely to come before the early 1990s, when large-scale fluidized-bed boilers or combined-cycle plants fueled by methane or gasified coal become commercially available. Even then, however, the greatest increases in power plant thermal efficiency will probably come from some of the smaller, modular technologies that will be competing with central station generating plants for a share of future electricity demand growth.

The economic slowdown: The overall slowdown in economic growth since the mid-1970s has also dramatically slowed utility sales and revenue growth. Real growth in GNP, which averaged about 4.0 percent a year from 1960 to 1972, fell to 2.7 percent per year during the period 1972 to 1981--a sizable drop. Meanwhile, the firm link that had characterized the relationship between energy demand growth and GNP growth before 1973 began to come uncoupled as rising energy prices encouraged a conservation ethic among energy consumers. In the high growth years of the 1960s, each 1 percent increase in real GNP was associated with almost a 2 percent increase in electricity demand. In the last decade, however, that ratio has fallen to about one to one. Thus, growth in demand for energy and fuels, including electricity, has fallen off even more rapidly than overall growth in GNP.

As noted earlier, average annual growth in utility kilowatt-hour sales and peak demand since 1973 has fallen to less than one-third the rate that prevailed before 1973. These growth rates have continued to deteriorate even further in recent years, with the industry experiencing peak demand growth of 0.3 percent and electricity sales growth of 1.2 percent in 1981 and negative growth in both categories in 1982. These trends are illustrated in Table 10, which shows annual percentage growth in GNP, utility peak demand and utility kilowatt-hour sales from 1970 through 1982.

Heightened competition: A final economic pressure that is beginning to have a significant impact on electric utilities is increased competition from a number of sources, including energy service companies, domestic and Canadian electric utilities and other forms of energy.

Table 10.

### Growth in GNP, Utility Industry Peak Demand, and Electricity Sales, 1970-82

| Year | GNP Growth (constant 1972 dollars) | Peak Demand Growth | Electricity Sales Growth (kwh) |
|------|------|------|------|
| 1970 | -0.2% | 6.6% | 5.9% |
| 1971 | 3.4 | 6.4 | 5.6 |
| 1972 | 5.7 | 9.2 | 7.6 |
| 1973 | 5.8 | 7.7 | 8.0 |
| 1974 | -0.6 | 1.3 | -0.1 |
| 1975 | -1.1 | 2.1 | 1.9 |
| 1976 | 5.4 | 4.0 | 6.7 |
| 1977 | 5.5 | 6.5 | 5.5 |
| 1978 | 4.8 | 3.3 | 3.4 |
| 1979 | 3.2 | 0.3 | 3.3 |
| 1980 | -0.2 | 4.8 | 2.0 |
| 1981 | 2.0 | 0.5 | 1.2 |
| 1982 | -1.9 | -3.5 | -2.7 |

SOURCES: U.S. Departments of Commerce and Energy, Electrical World.

For many years, individual electric utilities in the United States have been relatively insulated from competition by factors such as their territorial monopolies, regulated rates, a lack of foreign competition and the industry's cost structure and barriers to entry. Many of the characteristics of the electric utility industry that led to this lack of competition, however, have recently begun to break down.

Competition from energy service companies--Perhaps the greatest source of new competition now facing the industry is competition from conservation and energy service companies whose products reduce the need for central-station electric generation. As the declining marginal cost structure of the industry eroded during the 1970s, a host of new small scale power producers and energy efficiency and service companies have introduced products and technologies that compete with utility-supplied electricity. These companies range from industrial giants like General Electric and Atlantic Richfield to local contractors. Their products range from energy-efficient light bulbs and appliances to weatherstripping and industrial cogeneration units.

Considerable evidence suggests that the competition electric utilities face from small power producers and companies providing

energy services is really just beginning. Many of the products developed by U.S. companies as a result of the world "energy crises"
during the 1970s are just now reaching the market. In addition, recent regulatory and legal decisions, such as the Public Utility Regulatory Policies Act of 1978 (PURPA) and the June 1983 Supreme
Court decision upholding the interconnection and avoided cost principles of PURPA, have reduced substantially the regulatory uncertainties surrounding third-party power generation. Finally, foreign
manufacturers such as the Japanese and West Germans--who because
of their higher domestic energy prices have had a greater incentive
to develop energy-efficient products--appear poised to introduce a
slew of new energy-saving products into U.S. markets, further
stimulating domestic manufacturers in this area.

Exactly what form most of the new competition from energy
service companies will take remains to be seen. Various energy
planners and consultants have somewhat different perspectives on
this issue. John Alger, a General Electric program manager, tends to
see the question as big turbines versus small ones, both of which GE
can supply. "We sell big utility turbines and small turbines for third-
party producers. The question is, if the country is going to need 200
gigawatts of new capacity, will it be all big ones or will there be a lot
of small ones? Right now, it looks like there will be a fair amount of
these small ones." 33/ Peter Hunt, a Virginia-based energy consultant, sees Japan as a source of much of the new competition. "When
the Japanese start shipping in small, residential cogeneration units
about half the size of an icebox and selling them at a capital cost
equivalent of about $500 per kilowatt, I think you're going to see a
lot of people calling up their utilities and telling them to come get
their damn meters," says Hunt. "We may start seeing that in about
1988," he predicts. 34/

Other energy experts suggest that even cogeneration and small
scale electric generation look enormously expensive in comparison
with many of the energy-efficiency investments that have not yet
been made. Indeed, it appears that the recent drop in oil prices,
combined with the introduction of inexpensive microprocessors, is
ushering in a whole new wave of electricity-saving investments.
"We've been shifting our more expensive conservation efforts to gas
and electricity, and away from oil because of the relative paybacks
involved," notes Charles Feledy, director of corporate energy programs at United Technologies. 35/ And according to Robert H.
Williams, senior research physicist at Princeton University's Center
for Energy and Environmental Studies, such conservation efforts can
be expected to continue for some time:

> By focusing enormous resources on the development of
> power generation technology, we achieved a remarkable
> eight-fold improvement in the thermal efficiency of power
> generation between 1900 and 1960. Now, however, we are
> so high on this learning curve that it has become exceed-

ingly difficult to make further improvements. In contrast, second law efficiencies are quite low for most energy consuming activities, showing that the state of energy conservation technology is still very low on the learning curve-- roughly where electric power generation was near the turn of the century. Thus, with an adequate commitment to research and development in energy efficiency, we can expect significant new energy conservation opportunities to unfold for years to come. 36/

Competition among U.S. electric utilities--A second major source of heightened competition in the electric industry consists of competition among domestic electric utilities themselves brought on by changes in both the economic and the regulatory environment. This competition is already occurring in a number of forms. First, as reserve margins at many electric utilities have reached record levels, the incentive for utilities with excess capacity to market their surplus power has increased. This is leading to increased competition in the wholesale market--where utilities sell power to each other. It is also leading some utilities to advertise their rates in an attempt to attract industrial and commercial customers away from high-cost electric power areas such as New York City and Philadelphia. Second, the ancient competition between investor-owned and publicly owned utilities appears to be heating up again. Across the country, in places like Suffolk County New York and New Orleans, citizen groups are fighting to establish new municipal public power systems. Such systems appear attractive to many people because their tax exempt status, preferential access to low-cost federal hydroelectric power, and low overhead usually result in substantially lower electric rates to customers. In 1981, for instance, residential customers of investor-owned electric utilities paid an average of 43.5 percent more for each kWh of electricity than customers of publicly owned systems, while for commercial and industrial customers the difference was 30.7 percent. 37/

Much of the new impetus for the so-called "muni movement" appears to be coming from the steep rate increases imposed by investor-owned utilities as they bring new plants on line. On Long Island, for instance, opposition to large rate increases associated with the Shoreham nuclear plant is fueling a public power movement. "We see Long Island Lighting Co. as a private economic structure--that has made a lot of mistakes--set against the public interest," says Marjorie Harrison, chairman of the Long Island Public Power Project. 38/ Whether publicly owned systems are truly more efficient, or whether they are simply a conduit for tax subsidies, remains a heated topic of debate. Regardless, however, unless there are major changes in the laws governing publicly owned utilities, they are likely to present an ever greater source of competition for the investor-owned segment of the industry.

Competition with Canadian power--A third major source of

competition for some domestic electric utilities will be growing imports of excess Canadian power, primarily relatively low-cost hydroelectric power. Historically, Canada has developed its extensive hydroelectric resources primarily for domestic use and imported Canadian power has been a relatively insignificant factor in the overall U.S. power supply picture. In recent years, however, a glut of generating capacity has developed among Canadian utilities for many of the same reasons as it has among utilities in the United States. Meanwhile, because electric utilities in Canada are government-owned, there have been strong political and economic pressures not to reduce the level of new power plant construction, but rather to continue building new plants whose output will essentially be dedicated to the U.S. market. In addition to continuing to develop its hydroelectric resources, Canada recently began regulatory proceedings aimed at building a second nuclear unit at Point Lepreau, New Brunswick, whose output would be completely exported to the United States.

A surge in Canadian imports has already begun. Net imports of Canadian power to the United States more than tripled between 1976 and 1981 and now account for about 10 percent of electricity sales in New York and more than 5 percent in the New England states. 39/ Moreover, these levels are expected to continue increasing at a rapid rate over the next decade because a number of Canadian utilities-- particularly Hydro-Quebec, Ontario Hydro and British Columbia Hydro--face major surpluses of generating capacity and are committed to ambitious construction programs. "We see tremendous blocks of Canadian power available if we can find ways to bring it in at the right cost," says John Anderson, senior economist at the Electricity Consumers Resource Council, a group of major industrial energy users. 40/

In northern Quebec, Hydro-Quebec has embarked on a hydro-electric construction effort at James Bay that deserves particular attention. Five rivers have been diverted, more than 150 miles of earthen dikes and five major dams have been constructed and three huge reservoirs have been created to feed three enormous power stations. By early 1985, when the first phase of the project is completed, James Bay is expected to be capable of producing 10,000 megawatts of electricity, with subsequent phases planned to add as much as another 15,000 megawatts by the year 2000. Because this power is surplus to Canada's needs, financial success for the James Bay project now rests largely on power exports to the United States that were originally viewed as "icing on the cake," according to Richard Pouliot, Quebec's associate deputy minister of energy. 41/ The Canadian government has launched an aggressive push to peddle electricity south of the border that is meeting with some success. In 1982, Hydro-Quebec signed a contract to sell the Power Authority of the State of New York (PASNY) 111 billion kilowatt-hours over 13 years beginning in 1984. Then in March 1983, the company initialed an 11-year contract to sell some 33 billion kWh to the New England

Power Pool starting in 1986. Quebec Premier Rene Levesque her-
alded the latest agreement as "not only economically significant to us
in the northeast corner of the continent, but a very concrete example
of the economic patterns, especially in the area of trade, that are
drawing close neighbors even closer." 42/ Even with these sales,
however, Hydro-Quebec will be left with substantial surplus power.
If the subsequent stages of James Bay are completed, Hydro-Quebec
could supply enough power to meet 90 percent of New York State's
new demand for the rest of the century according to Pouliot. "Power
from Quebec would cost less than anything that can be built in the
U.S.," adds Pierre Bolduc, Hydro-Quebec's treasurer. 43/ Hydro-
Quebec is now reported to be searching for customers further south
in New Jersey, Pennsylvania and Maryland.

<u>Competition with other energy sources</u>--A final source of in-
creased competition facing electric utilities comes from other energy
sources, particularly natural gas and some of the renewables. Over
the last decade, electric utilities have made considerable progress in
penetrating certain markets that had been held by other energy
sources. These include consumer appliances, space heating, HVAC
equipment and certain industrial processes. Rising electricity prices
are now providing market opportunities for other energy sources to
regain lost markets. Passive solar heating is already beginning to
take an increasing share of residential and commercial space heating
markets. Meanwhile, gas utilities are gearing up to counterattack
electricity in some industrial markets and to enter electric power
markets through the back door, by selling gas-fueled power production devices ranging from cogeneration systems to fuel cells.

Exactly what form most of the new competition electric utilities
face in the 1980s remains open to question. There is little doubt,
however, that such new competition will exist. "The size of the total
energy pie is not growing rapidly, and the name of the game is becoming 'share of market'," notes energy consultant Richard Metzler.
"We will see much more competition between electricity and gas,
between investor-owned and publicly owned utilities, and between
geographic regions." 44/

## Pressures from Regulation and the Politicization of Utility Planning

In addition to pressures resulting from basic changes in its economic environment, the utility industry faces a number of pressures
from specific groups and from the general politicization of the utility
decisionmaking process. These pressures emanate from at least four
major sources--regulators, ratepayers, stockholders and the financial
community, and special interest activist groups. The concerns and
objectives of each of these constituents differ and in many instances
conflict, but actions taken by each have contributed to the strategic
and financial pressures facing the industry.

Regulators: Probably the greatest source of political pressure on the industry results from regulation. This pressure comes in three distinct forms, all of which are having a major financial impact. First, health, safety and environmental regulations aimed at the electric utility industry have clearly had a profound effect in driving up utility costs. Federal and, to a lesser extent, state environmental and safety regulations were a significant factor in the dramatic increases in utility construction, operating and maintenance, and fuel costs discussed earlier in this chapter. It is estimated that during the 1970s, for instance, new regulatory requirements for nuclear plants approximately doubled the amounts of labor, materials, and equipment and tripled the design engineering effort required for each new unit of nuclear capacity. 45/ Federal nuclear plant safety regulations have also greatly increased costs for operator training, emergency planning, security, radiation protection and a host of other O&M costs and have reduced the maximum allowed power level at some reactors afflicted with steam generator corrosion, reactor containment embrittlement or other generic problems.

Regulations governing power plant emissions stand out as another area where environmental regulation has had an enormous financial impact. A recent study by Data Resources found that utilities will have spent $101 billion on the purchase, operation and maintenance of air and water pollution control equipment between 1970 and 1987--a regulatory burden that easily exceeds that of any other industry. 46/ At coal- and oil-fired plants, operation of stack-gas scrubbing equipment also reduces thermal efficiency, requiring additional fuel consumption. Finally, regulations affecting coal and uranium mining, handling and transportation have been a significant factor in the increased cost of those fuels.

The direct cost impact of such past and future regulatory requirements for four representative electric utilities was documented in a 1981 report by the General Accounting Office. As shown in Table 11, increased costs resulted from utility compliance with a broad range of agency regulations.

To some extent, utilities have also been whipsawed by federal regulatory efforts based on national security considerations. Federal regulations during the 1970s honed in on the utility industry's heavy dependence on imported oil, banning the construction of new large oil-burning plants and discouraging use of existing oil- and gas-fired plants. Utilities were exhorted to build new coal-fired or nuclear plants to replace their oil- or gas-fired capacity or to convert existing oil-fired plants to coal. Now, with nuclear and coal plant capital costs skyrocketing and the price of oil falling, the financial wisdom of a number of these projects is increasingly questionable. Energy pundits on Capitol Hill are already predicting that within the next several years, Congress will overturn the off-gas provisions of the Powerplant and Industrial Fuel Use Act of 1978--which directs electric utilities to cease burning natural gas in base-load plants by 1990. Moreover, it appears likely that the unresolved environmental

Table 11.

## Actual/Estimated Regulatory Costs
## For Four Utility Companies - By Agency

| | | Costs | | |
|---|---|---|---|---|
| **Table Actual/Estimated Regulatory Costs for Four Utility Companies — By Agency** | | | | |
| **Agency** | **Number of regulatory examples** | **Actual capital** | **Estimated annual recurring** | **Estimated future** |
| | | (in millions) | | |
| Environmental Protection Agency | 36 | $473.56 | $57.89 | a/$194.00 |
| Nuclear Regulatory Commission | 10 | 43.79 | —0— | b/409.82 |
| Occupational Safety and Health Administration | 9 | .45 | .07 | c/4.47 |
| Securities and Exchange Commission | 5 | 1.12 | .03 | —0— |
| Federal Energy Regulatory Commission | 7 | 6.77 | 1.47 | —0— |
| Corps of Engineers | 4 | 41.78 | —0— | —0— |
| Department of the Interior | 4 | 1.66 | —0— | —0— |
| Equal Employment Opportunity Commission | 2 | .15 | .13 | —0— |
| State regulations | 16 | 83.20 | d/49.73 | e/155.00 |
| Total | 93 | $652.48 | $109.32 | $763.29 |

a/  Costs for installing flue gas scrubbers.
b/  Increased power costs resulting from construction delays caused by intervenor actions.
c/  Contingent upon implementation of proposed standards.
d/  Expected annual cost differential resulting from the use of low-sulfur oil from 1980 to 2000.
e/  Expected cost differential of the increased use of oil which is attributable to a 14-month delay in construction.

SOURCE:   U.S. General Accounting Office, "The Effects of Regulation on the Electric Utility Industry."

issues posed by greater use of nuclear and coal plants may come back to haunt these electricity sources, resulting in a continuing series of new environmental regulations and added costs to utilities. Some analysts have even suggested that these new regulatory pressures will be great enough to pressure some utilities to convert back to oil or gas. Dayton Power & Light, for instance, proposed in November 1983 that the stalled Zimmer nuclear plant be converted to a gas-fired plant after Zimmer co-owner Cincinnati Gas & Electric announced a $2 billion increase in the plant's estimated cost. In January 1984, Cincinnati Gas opted to convert the plant to a coal-fired unit. 47/

Similarly, national security concerns about nuclear proliferation during the Ford and Carter administrations led them to prohibit the reprocessing of nuclear spent fuel--the utility industry's preferred solution to the nuclear waste problem--imposing new costs on utilities that had not planned for long-term on-site waste storage.

Finally, national security and balance of trade considerations, or at least the rhetoric associated with these issues, may play a large role in determining the levels of electricity imports that the United States will allow from Canada in the mid-1980s and beyond. The Bonneville Power Administration, a federal agency, is already concerned that efforts by British Columbia Hydro to market surplus Canadian hydro capacity to California may undercut BPA's own efforts to sell power to California.

A second pressure on electric utilities arising from regulation is the tendency of some state public utility commissions to hold rate increases to a minimum. While some state regulators have recently begun to grant large rate increases and there has been an upward trend in the authorized rate of return for most utilities, it is clear that the regulatory process in many states remains highly politicized. "Electricity is perhaps the most politicized of all energy sources," notes Clyde Greenert, energy policy manager for Union Carbide. "The problem . . . is that there is no free market or alternative and, thus, the job of seeking equilibrium between producers and consumers is totally a political one." 48/ One indication of this regulatory pressure on utility earnings is that the actual return on equity for the electric utility industry hovered near 11 percent for the last decade, a rate below the return available from competing investments and below the cost of acquiring new capital for virtually all utilities. While responsibility for lagging utility earnings certainly does not rest solely with the regulators--indeed many observers argue that the industry has compiled a record for poor forecasting in recent years that is virtually without equal among major U.S. industries--it is nevertheless true that state utility commission rate decisions substantially weakened the financial condition of the industry during the 1970s. "The political environment in which PUCs operate virtually ensures that commissioners will opt for a strategy of short-run rate suppression at the expense of medium- and long-term benefits to both ratepayers and utilities," says Peter Navarro, a researcher at Harvard University's Energy and Environmental Policy Center. 49/

A final pressure on utilities involving regulation stems from the gradual usurpation of utilities' decisionmaking powers by state regulators. As state regulators have beefed up their staffs with economists and started to do their own forecasting--and as demand forecasts by some utilities have continued to fly in the face of reality--a number of state regulatory commissions have become much more aggressive about injecting their own decisions into the utility planning process. Decisions that once were solely in the hands of utility managers--such as whether to build a new generating unit, what type of unit to build, and where to build it--have increasingly become subject to regulatory review and veto. "We're looking over their shoulders more," notes Alan R. Erwin, chairman of the Texas Public Utilities Commission. 50/ Recently, for instance, utility commissions in at least two states--Pennsylvania and New Hampshire--have attempted to force the termination of half-built nuclear plants by denying the utilities involved--Philadelphia Electric and Public Service of New Hampshire--permission to finance the units. In California, where the state energy commission is required by law to prepare its own demand forecast for comparison with utility forecasts, the commission has used its own staff's lower forecasts for rate-making purposes, citing weaknesses in the utilities' forecasts. And in several states--including New York, New Jersey and Connecticut--regulators have begun to move toward the use of incentive/penalty mechanisms that limit the exposure of ratepayers to nuclear plant cost overruns by placing ceilings on the amount of individual plant costs that can be included in a company's rate base. Utility managers are thus becoming constrained in their ability to implement construction plans and demand management programs based on their own business judgments.

Because this situation is relatively new, it remains uncertain what impact it will ultimately have on the financial prospects of electric utilities. The evidence to date suggests a mixed record for regulatory intervention into the utility planning process. Federal subsidies and regulatory intervention largely created the civilian nuclear power program--a decidedly mixed blessing for utilities--and were largely responsible for forcing many utilities to convert from coal to oil in the 1960s--a disaster in view of subsequent actions by OPEC. Now federal pressure is a factor in pushing utilities toward conversion or replacement of oil- and gas-burning facilities with coal--a decision that may further hammer some utilities if current research efforts into the problems of acid rain and carbon dioxide buildup indicate the need for massive coal cleanup programs or a shift away from coal burning altogether. State intervention, on the other hand, is a much newer phenomenon and appears often to have had the effect of preventing construction of new power plants that, in retrospect, were not needed.

Ratepayers: A second major source of political pressure on utilities comes from ratepayers--the residential, commercial and industrial customers that buy electric power. Utility ratepayers exert political pressure in several ways. First, they lobby against rate increases in proceedings before state regulatory commissions. "The ratepayer, recognizing a politically vulnerable target, is literally 'going after' the companies, regulators and legislators," says Kenneth Hollister of Dean Witter Reynolds. 51/ In many cases, these efforts appear to have had a very significant impact in holding down utility rate increases, especially in states where regulators are elected by the public rather than appointed. "States that have elected commissions starve the utilities," says John Slatter, utility analyst at Prescott, Ball & Turben. 52/ Ratepayers also lobby for legislative changes to increase consumer involvement in the utility planning and ratemaking processes. "Since the costs of resources began going up . . . we have seen the creation of organized ratepayer groups," notes Robert

McKinney, president of the American Public Power Association. "Consumers, in general, are taking a more active interest in all their utilities." 53/

Ratepayer lobbying efforts are virtually certain to grow as a result of rate hikes and greater nationwide interest in citizen utility boards--or CUBs as they are known. CUBs are independent membership organizations authorized by state legislatures to give consumers a stronger voice at hearings on utility rate increase and legislative proposals. They operate by soliciting funds through insertions in monthly utility bills, polling ratepayers, and then hiring lawyers, consultants and lobbyists to speak for consumer interests. Ralph Nader originated the concept in 1974, but it has only recently begun to gain widespread attention. In Wisconsin, the nation's first CUB opened its doors in November 1979 and claims to have helped cut $100 million of utility rate increase requests in that state. A second CUB was formed in Illinois in 1983 and proponents are now pushing for CUBs in 20 other states. 54/ "People are now more concerned about utility rates than taxes," contends State Sen. Vince Demuzio of Illinois. 55/

Finally, utility ratepayers are beginning to exercise yet another mechanism for influencing electric companies--the public referendum. To date, ratepayers have used public referenda principally as a means of opposing further nuclear power development. A number of states have passed ballot proposals that severely restrict future nuclear plant construction, radioactive waste disposal and transportation, and uranium mining. California, for instance, has passed a series of initiatives that make further nuclear plant construction in that state highly unlikely, while voters in Massachusetts have approved an initiative that will require voter and state legislature approval to site a nuclear plant or nuclear waste disposal facility in that state. In the last several years, however, voters have begun to focus on broader issues affecting electric utility planning and regulation. In 1981, voters in the state of Washington approved a ballot initiative that requires voter approval before any public agency can issue bonds to finance the construction of large generating plants. The initiative could signal the end for public tolerance of fiscal disasters like the Washington Public Power Supply System's ambitious nuclear construction program in that state. But as Vic Reinemer, editor of Public Power, notes, "The controversy in the Northwest goes beyond the nuclear and cost issue to two other substantial points, central generation and degree of public participation in decisionmaking." 56/ And in 1982, petition campaigns to require ballot initiatives on the election of public utility commissioners were successful in bringing the issue to a vote in Ohio and Michigan--although the initiatives failed in both states.

Overall, there is a trend toward more public participation in the utility planning process--especially in cases where public funds are used--and toward a direct public veto mechanism over the use of controversial technologies, particularly nuclear power. "People are

Figure 4.

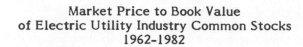

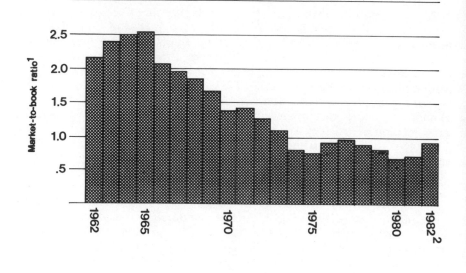

Market Price to Book Value
of Electric Utility Industry Common Stocks
1962-1982

[1]Average of high and low value for year
[2]August 1982

SOURCE:    Utility Compustat.


going to continue to be unhappy with utility rates, and that leads to agitation for change," says Walter French, a utility analyst with Argus Research Corp. "They think a different system would be better than the current one." 57/

Stockholders and Wall Street: A third major source of political and financial pressure on the industry in recent years has been electric utility stockholders and the financial community. As the industry's financial problems became apparent during the 1970s, utility stockholders responded in two ways--"exit" and "voice." Many chose to utilize the exit option by selling their utility stockholdings in favor of other investments. Investor disenchantment with electric utility stocks during the 1970s is evidenced by the continuing decline in the market price to book value ratio of electric utility common stocks shown in Figure 4. During this period, a significant percentage of institutional investors reduced their holdings of utility common stocks or eliminated them altogether.

Many investors, including large institutions, began to return to electric utility common stock investments in 1982 because of the drop in interest rates and the high dividend yield of most utility stocks. The market-to-book ratio for electric utility common stocks reached 94 percent at the end of 1982 and briefly flirted with 100 percent in early 1983, according to Dick Braacz, vice president for finance at the Edison Electric Institute. But according to Braacz, "The improvement in the market-to-book ratio for utility stocks is more a function of the decline in interest rates and the bullish stock market than of fundamental improvement in the industry's financial situation." 58/ Moreover, many of the institutional investors buying utility stocks in recent years say they view these stocks primarily as dividend and trading vehicles rather than as long-term investments.

Perhaps equally as significant as utility stock sales, however, is the fact that utility stockholders have increasingly exercised the "voice" option available through stock ownership. Stockholders are increasingly challenging utility decisions through criticism of management at company annual meetings, through lawsuits, and through submission of shareholder resolutions aimed at changing company policies. As with the public referendum process, the focal point of utility shareholder activism in recent years has been the issue of nuclear power development. But both the number of shareholder proposals submitted to utilities and the range of issues they cover are expanding. More than 100 shareholder proposals dealing with social responsibility questions were voted on at electric utility annual meetings in the three-year period 1981-1983, up from only 36 in the period 1977-80. 59/ In addition, utility shareholders have begun challenging utility managements on issues such as the development of conservation and alternative energy programs, the operating efficiency of fossil fuel plants, the competence of company management and the dilution of shareholders' equity through the issuance of common stock below book value.

Although the record suggests that utility shareholders are not likely to force dramatic changes in utility policies through the passage of shareholder proposals--no shareholder proposal on a social responsibility question opposed by management has ever passed--the behind-the-scenes effect of shareholder activism on the utility planning process cannot be easily dismissed. On average, shareholder resolutions to utilities on energy issues receive some of the highest levels of support of any shareholder proposals. Moreover, on at least two occasions in recent years, utility managements supported--and stockholders subsequently approved--shareholder proposals calling for substantive changes in previous business practices. In 1981, a resolution approved at Public Service of Colorado directed the company's board of directors to "use every available means, consistent with maintaining the financial integrity of the company, to stop diluting the equity of our common stock, including but not limited to seeking further rate increases and reducing operating costs and capital spending." 60/ And in 1982, a resolution passed at Central Maine

Power directing the company to "pursue a general policy favoring renewable energy, conservation and decentralization" of power generation facilities. 61/ In addition, an increasing number of utilities are adopting the energy supply strategy predominantly favored by shareholder activists--the shifting of new capital investment away from new nuclear and coal-fired generation to the development of energy conservation programs and renewable energy technologies.

In addition to greater use of the shareholder resolution process, a few utility shareholders have begun to use lawsuits in an attempt to alter utility financing practices that they see as detrimental to existing shareholders. William Norgren, for instance, a large shareholder of Pacific Gas & Electric, recently sued the utility and the California Public Utilities Commission charging that the continuing sale of the utility's stock at prices below book value constituted a confiscation of property that violates his civil rights. Early in 1982, Norgren was instrumental in blocking an issue of 1.5 million common shares by Idaho Power. "I'm not anti-management or anti-utility," Norgren stated. "But where there is repetitive, ongoing dilutive financing, then there is a liability on the part of both utility boards of directors and utility commissions." 62/

The financial community has also played an important role in pressuring electric utilities. Although utility stocks and bonds have garnered growing support from financial analysts since early 1982 as investments that should benefit from falling interest rates and "disinflation," analysts' general assessments of electric utility industry common stocks and utility managements have been negative for many years. Most electric utilities have seen their bond and preferred stock ratings downgraded over the last decade. According to Anne Faber, vice president for rates and regulation at Standard & Poor's Corp., the percentage of utility companies with 'A' or better bond ratings fell from 96 percent in 1970 to 67 percent in 1980 while the category of 'BBB' or lower grew from 4 percent to 33 percent in the same time frame. 63/ As Table 12 indicates, the trend toward downgradings in the industry has still not ended, although a significant minority of electric utilities are now beginning to improve their ratings.

The ratings on some utilities' bonds have fallen so low that many institutional investors are prohibited by law from buying them because they are not considered to be of investment quality. A number of brokerage firms, including Merrill Lynch, have also issued reports questioning the need for the ambitious construction programs of some utilities and advocating the abandonment of a number of large generating plants now under construction.

Such actions by Wall Street can be seen more as a reflection of the utility industry's financial problems than as a direct cause of them, of course. Nevertheless, moves by the financial community in response to the deterioration in the financial condition of the utility industry have increased the cost of new capital for the industry and are requiring utility executives to expend far greater amounts of

Table 12.

### Electric Utility Senior Debt Rating Changes by Moody's
### 1971-1983

| Year | Number of Ratings | |
|---|---|---|
| | Lowered | Increased |
| 1971 | 3 | 1 |
| 1972 | 3 | 1 |
| 1973 | 2 | 3 |
| 1974 | 25 | 1 |
| 1975 | 15 | 2 |
| 1976 | 9 | 0 |
| 1977 | 2 | 3 |
| 1978 | 4 | 1 |
| 1979 | 6 | 3 |
| 1980 | 14 | 1 |
| 1981 | 8 | 1 |
| 1982 | 17 | 12 |
| 1983 (March 31) | 3 | 0 |

SOURCES: White Weld & Co., Edison Electric Institute

time on financing matters than they have in the past. The ascendance of financial concerns at electric utilities has been so great that leadership of the industry--which has traditionally rested with executives with engineering backgrounds--appears to be passing to executives with financial backgrounds. Utility shareholders and Wall Street, it appears, are beginning to join regulators, ratepayers and special interest groups in the quest for greater participation in the utility planning process.

Special interest groups: A final source of pressure on utility managements comes from what might be called the organized anti-nuclear, environmental and consumer movements. This grouping includes a wide variety of organizations with diverse and sometimes conflicting interests. Anti-nuclear groups include local or regional organizations such as the Clamshell Alliance, Abalone Alliance and SHAD Alliance that oppose a particular power plant, as well as groups like the Union of Concerned Scientists that do research on nuclear safety issues and lobby for legislation to tighten nuclear regulation. Environmental groups include such organizations as the Environmental Defense Fund, Natural Resources Defense Council, Friends of the Earth, Sierra Club, Citizens for a Better Environment and Environmental Policy Center that engage in a variety of research, lobbying and litigation activities to support environmental protection laws, encourage energy conservation and oppose power plant construction. Consumer groups include organizations such as Toward Utility Rate Normalization (TURN) and Massachusetts Fair Share--that try to keep residential electric rates as low as possible --as well as groups such as ACORN that emphasize the particular needs of low-income consumers through support for "lifeline" rates and restrictions on utility shutoffs.

Throughout the 1970s, these various special interest groups became increasingly able to challenge utility decisions about nuclear plant safety, coal mining practices, the need for rate increases and a host of other issues in the courts, in testimony before regulatory authorities and at demonstrations at utility construction sites. It remains difficult to assess the overall impact that such intervention has had on the utility planning process. Some groups were notably successful in attaining their objectives; others were not. It seems safe to say, however, that the impact these groups had in slowing nuclear power development, in lobbying for various regulations governing coal use and in halting development of the breeder reactor in the United States was enormous. Litigation over environmental laws was a primary factor in delaying a number of nuclear projects to the extent they were deemed no longer economic by the utilities building them and canceled.

While the issues that these groups focus on in the 1980s may change--a number of major environmental groups now consider nuclear power to be a dead issue and are beginning to concentrate on other areas, such as nuclear disarmament and acid rain--it seems clear that environmental and other special interest groups will continue to be active on questions affecting the utility industry. And with the expertise developed by these groups during the last decade, it seems plausible that their ability to persuade the courts, regulatory authorities and the public on issues affecting utilities may be as significant during the 1980s as it was during the 1970s.


### The Overall Impact:  Weakened Utilities Facing a New Business Environment

This chapter has discussed a number of the economic, political and social pressures that electric utilities confronted during the 1970s and continue to face today. The following sections analyze the overall impact of these pressures on the industry's financial condition and business environment.

Deterioration of financial condition:  The most obvious impact of inflation, escalating costs, and mounting political and social pressures on the industry is a marked deterioration in its financial condition. No one disputes that this deterioration has occurred--although utility officials tend to blame it on poor regulation while critics see it as evidence of tough economic times and bad management. "By the usual Wall Street indexes, the electric utility industry is a financial invalid, and a transfusion of dollars is needed to get it out of bed and back to any reasonable definition of financial health," says Irwin Stelzer, president of National Economic Research Associates Inc. 64/ During the decade of the 1970s, the industry's costs rose by more than $50 billion over and above the proportional increase in electric plants in service. 65/ The result was an ever-increasing flow of requests and approvals for rate increases, as shown in Table 13. Moreover, although many observers note that utility rate increases in percentage terms are falling, on an inflation-adjusted basis, these increases have accelerated in recent years, as is illustrated in Table 14.

The flood of rate increases that began in the mid-1970s has done little to aid utility investors or the financial condition of the industry, except perhaps to prevent greater deterioration than actually occurred. Although the industry's net earnings nearly tripled during the 1970s, the average share of electric utility stock lost value during the decade even without considering the effects of inflation. 66/ Utility analyst Charles Benore of Paine, Webber, Mitchell and Hutchins noted in 1981 that investors had made money in only four out of the last 15 years on electric utility common stock. 67/ In addition, utility dividends—frequently touted as the major attraction of utility stocks—were unable to achieve a rate of growth that exceeded the inflation rate. One study of utility dividend growth for the period 1965-78 found that of 74 electric utilities, only six were able to raise dividends rapidly enough to compensate for inflation. 68/ On average, utility dividends grew at only two-thirds of the inflation rate for the period. "Electric industry shareholders have taken a terrible whipping in the last 10 years," concludes Frank Griffith, chairman of the Edison Electric Institute. 69/

For utility companies themselves, the financial consequences of the 1970s were equally bleak. Burgeoning capital requirements made it impossible to finance expansion out of net earnings. Total net income for the industry has averaged less than 37 percent of total capital expenditures since 1970. 70/ Moreover, the quality of utility earnings has deteriorated markedly because a rising proportion of the industry's reported earnings are in "non-cash" accounting entries, especially the "allowance for funds used during construction," or AFUDC. AFUDC credits utility net income with an imputed return on funds tied up in new construction, aiding utility income statements but not providing any cash flow. As shown in Table 15, the AFUDC component of utility earnings grew from 12.9 percent in 1969 to 46.9 percent in 1982, according to the Edison Electric Institute. Preliminary EEI estimates suggest that AFUDC could account for as much as 56 percent of earnings in 1983. "The industry's 'cash' earnings since 1975 have not even been adequate to meet dividend payments on common stock, much less help fund construction costs," notes economist Arthur Thompson. "Even when all other sources of

Table 13.

## Electric Utility Rate Applications and Approvals
## 1970-1982
(millions of dollars)

| Year | Number of Rate Increases Filed | Amounts Requested | Amounts Approved |
|------|-------------------------------|-------------------|------------------|
| 1970 | 80  | $   797 | $   533 |
| 1971 | 113 | 1,368   | 826   |
| 1972 | 110 | 1,205   | 853   |
| 1973 | 139 | 2,125   | 1,089 |
| 1974 | 212 | 4,555   | 2,229 |
| 1975 | 191 | 3,973   | 3,094 |
| 1976 | 169 | 3,747   | 2,275 |
| 1977 | 162 | 3,953   | 2,311 |
| 1978 | 154 | 4,494   | 2,419 |
| 1979 | 178 | 5,736   | 2,853 |
| 1980 | 254 | 10,871  | 5,932 |
| 1981 | 237 | 11,902  | 8,341 |
| 1982 | 230 | 11,920  | 7,630 |

SOURCE:   Edison Electric Institute

Table 14.

## Electric Utility Percentage Rate Increases
(nominal and real)

| Year | Nominal | Real |
|------|---------|------|
| 1978 | 7.3%  | -1.6% |
| 1979 | 8.1   | -4.6  |
| 1980 | 17.9  | 4.9   |
| 1981 | 14.7  | 5.3   |
| 1982 | 12.0  | 7.0   |

SOURCE:   Charles M. Studness, Public Utilities Fortnightly.

Table 15.

### AFUDC as a Percent of Net Income
### Investor-Owned Electric Utility Industry
### 1969-82

| Year | AFUDC (a) (millions) | Net Income (b) (millions) | AFUDC as % of Net Income |
|------|------|------|------|
| 1969 | $    405 | $   3,130 | 12.9% |
| 1970 | 594 | 3,333 | 17.8 |
| 1971 | 822 | 3,774 | 21.8 |
| 1972 | 1,095 | 4,356 | 25.1 |
| 1973 | 1,297 | 4,851 | 26.7 |
| 1974 | 1,596 | 5,146 | 31.0 |
| 1975 | 1,694 | 6,002 | 28.2 |
| 1976 | 1,896 | 6,990 | 27.1 |
| 1977 | 2,367 | 7,813 | 30.3 |
| 1978 | 2,907 | 8,574 | 33.9 |
| 1979 | 3,727 | 9,302 | 40.1 |
| 1980 | 4,627 | 10,524 | 44.0 |
| 1981 | 5,489 | 12,658 | 43.4 |
| 1982 | 7,009 | 14,955 | 46.9 |

(a)   AFUDC includes both borrowed and equity funds for all years.
(b)   Before preferred dividends.

SOURCE:   Edison Electric Institute

internal funds are included, most companies still have had nowhere near a sufficient internal cash flow to pay construction costs," Thompson adds. "The industry's ratio of internal cash flow to actual construction outlays averaged 33 percent during the 1970s." 71/ As a consequence of their heavy capital spending, electric utilities became very dependent on external sources of capital. During the 1970s, the investor-owned segment of the industry raised $111.7 billion in new external capital--including $61.8 billion in new long-term bonds, $27.9 billion from common stock issuances, $17.5 billion from new issues of preferred stock and $4.5 billion in short-term bank loans. 72/ This trend toward greater use of external financing has also accelerated so far in the 1980s.

The extensive need for external financing by electric utilities, coupled with rising interest rates and lagging earnings growth, has resulted in severe erosion of the industry's earnings coverage ratios and credit ratings. For the industry overall, interest coverage ratios

Figure 5.

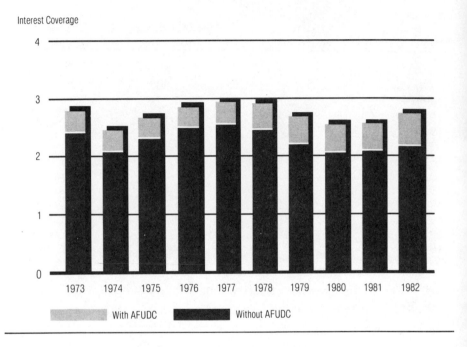

### Interest Coverage of Investor-owned Electric Utilities
### (Before Federal Income Taxes)
### 1973-82

SOURCE:   Edison Electric Institute, "Financial Review - 1982"

on mortgage bonds—the ratio of earnings to fixed charges--have deteriorated dramatically from the levels of the 1960s, when they were
generally in the 4.0 times to 6.0 times range. As shown in Figure 5,
in 1980, the industry's interest coverage ratio stood at 2.5 times,
about equal to its level in the crisis year of 1974, when Con Edison
omitted its dividend.  Since 1980, the utility industry's interest coverage has improved somewhat, rising to 2.72 times at the end of
1982. 73/  Nevertheless, some electric utilities have at times found
themselves without the necessary coverage to issue new mortgage
bonds or preferred stock, forcing costly delays or cancellations of
financings and construction projects.  With the debt markets becoming increasingly expensive as sources for new capital, utilities have
recently resorted to more frequent and larger issuances of new common stock.  But with many electric utility stocks still selling at substantial discounts from book value, this practice has resulted in

Figure 6.

### Electric Utility Bond Ratings, 1970 and 1982

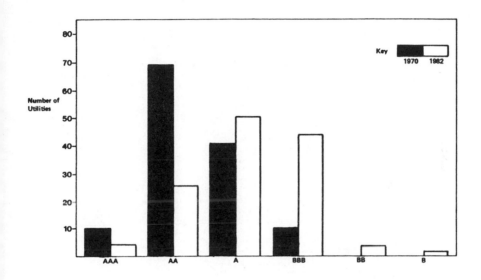

SOURCE:   Standard & Poor's Bond Guide.

significant dilution of shareholders' equity and is now engendering growing criticism from utility investors and stock analysts. Overall, there has been a marked deterioration in the creditworthiness of electric utilities that has dramatically limited utilities' flexibility in selecting the type and timing of their financing programs. This trend is illustrated in Figure 6, which compares the credit ratings of major electric utilities in 1970 and 1982.

High rates diminish growth prospects: While it is clear that the rate increases granted to electric utilities in the 1970s were inadequate to better the financial positions of the utilities and their investors and finance the massive construction effort that utility executives embarked on, it is equally evident that these rate increases have had a significant effect on electricity consumption habits. As illustrated in Figure 7, beginning in 1973 a fundamental change took place in the direction of average electricity prices. Since 1973, the price of

Figure 7.

### Average Price of Electricity
### Sold by the Electric Utility Industry to End-Use Sectors
### 1960-1982

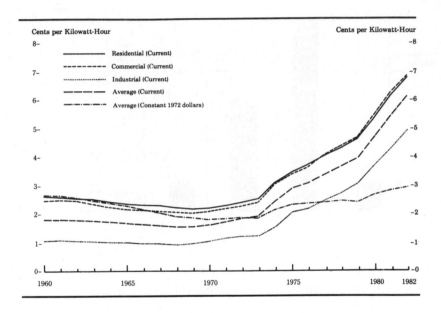

SOURCE:   Energy Information Administration, "1982 Annual Energy
          Review."

electricity has risen at an annual rate of 13.7 percent in current
dollars and 5.5 percent in constant dollars. 74/
    Industry executives now agree that in the past they seriously
underestimated the degree of consumer responsiveness to electricity
price increases. "We've found [demand for] our product a lot less
inelastic than we thought," says Richard Korpan, vice president for
finance at San Diego Gas & Electric. 75/  But there is still relatively
little agreement among industry analysts and planners as to the

Table 16.

### Surveys of Own-Price Elasticity for Electricity
### (long run)

|                        | Residential Sector | Industrial Sector |
| ---------------------- | ------------------ | ----------------- |
| Taylor a/ (8 studies)  | -0.90 to -2.0      | -1.25 to -1.94    |
| MRG b/ (3 studies)     | -0.78 to -1.66     | -0.69 to -1.03    |
| Pindyck c/ (4 studies) | -0.3 to -1.2       | -0.5 to -0.92     |

SOURCES:
a/ L.D. Taylor, "The Demand for Electricity: A Survey," The Bell Journal of Economics 6, no. 1 (Spring 1975).
b/ Modeling Resources Group, CONAES, Energy Modeling for an Uncertain Future (Washington, D.C.: National Research Council, 1978).
c/ R. Pindyck, "The Characteristics of Energy Demand," in J. Sawhill ed. Energy Conservation and Public Policy (Englewood Cliffs, N.J.: Prentice-Hall, 1979).

extent to which consumers will take additional conservation measures in response to past and future increases in electricity prices. The substantial range of uncertainty concerning estimates of the long-run price elasticity of demand for electricity is reflected in the meta-survey in Table 16--a survey of the surveys of elasticity studies. 76/

Current estimates by the utility industry predict peak-load growth of about 3 percent per year for the next 10 years, assuming an average GNP growth rate of 2 to 3 percent. 77/ Many government and private forecasters believe that, if anything, this forecast is too low. "Most forecasters are probably underestimating demand growth because of low GNP estimates," says ICF Inc.'s Robert Spann, who believes that GNP estimates "tend to be a lagging indicator." 78/ But a growing minority of forecasters are saying that such estimates are pipe dreams. Houston-based Planning and Forecasting Consultants Inc., for instance, maintains that "U.S. electricity consumption will have a negative growth rate for the rest of the decade." 79/ Similarly, Energy Ventures Analysis of Arlington, Va., recently analyzed the annual load forecasts of all U.S. utilities and concluded that "the utilities are still overforecasting." The consulting firm stated that "some large utilities are offering good numbers, but a lot of utilities are still submitting bad stuff, using old-fashioned trend-line numbers," and that many additional nuclear and coal-fired power plants would be deferred or canceled. 80/

New perceptions about the business environment: The weakened financial condition and slowing demand growth that the electric utility industry has experienced may be most significant as symptoms of much broader changes that have taken place in the industry's operating environment. A number of the industry's financial indicators have begun to recover in 1983 as the overall economy has improved, and many industry observers believe that the worst is now over for the industry. "Overall, the financial health of America's utilities is improving gradually. I suspect this results primarily from a happy combination of sophisticated management, creative engineering, and productive employees," says Donald McCarthy, chairman and CEO of Northern States Power Co. 81/ "With slower demand growth and improved cash positions, I see a gradual transition that is primarily beneficial to the industry," adds Michael Foley, director of financial analysis for the National Association of Regulatory Utility Commissioners. 82/

But while there is no consensus on the subject, there is considerable evidence that the financial slump plaguing much of the industry is not solely the product of cyclical economic factors or one-time shocks like the quadrupling of oil prices in 1974. "The industry still has to contend with conflicting corporate objectives--providing consumers electricity at least cost, ensuring adequate returns to shareholders, and juggling various public policy requirements," notes Eric Zausner, senior vice president at Booz, Allen & Hamilton. "As a result, the rest of this decade really won't be much better than the 1970s, which may have been the worst of times for utilities," Zausner predicts. 83/ "The electrical utility industry's long-term fundamentals continue to be unfavorable," adds Ernest Liu, a utility analyst for Goldman, Sachs. 84/ Overall, it is clear that the industry is becoming less homogeneous and that broad brush generalizations about the industry's financial health are becoming less meaningful than in the past. Some utilities with abundant low-cost generating sources are literally becoming "cash cows" with the only problem being how to invest their excess cash flow profitably. Others, however--and this portion of the industry is considerably larger than many people generally assume--remain mired with problems that could eventually end in multiple bankruptcies and corporate reorganizations.

Utility managers and critics alike are arriving at the conclusion that the industry must adapt to fundamental changes in its general business environment--changes with important strategic ramifications for utility executives and regulators. "The financial problems facing the electric utility industry have accelerated so rapidly in recent years that many in the industry believe that there must be a substantive change in the way in which utilities conduct their businesses," states Lelan F. Sillin, chairman and chief executive officer of Northeast Utilities. 85/ A number of the most important changes in the industry's operating environment are outlined below.

## Environment for U.S. Electric Utilities

|  | Historical (pre-1970) | Recent Past (1970-1982) |
|---|---|---|
| Load growth | High, predictable | Low, unpredictable |
| Technology | Steadily improving | Little improvement |
| Economies of scale | Substantial | Limited |
| Fuel costs | Declining | Rapid increases |
| Favored technologies | Coal, oil and gas, hydro | Coal and nuclear |
| Regulatory environment | Supportive | Unsupportive |
| Financial condition | Strong | Weak |
| Promotional activities | Aggressive | Limited |

In summary, while there is growing agreement among utilities, their critics and industry regulators that something must change if the industry is to regain its financial health, there remain distinct differences of opinion about the primary source of the industry's problems and the appropriate business strategy for responding to those problems. Thus, segments of the industry appear to be following broadly diverging courses based on differing perceptions about the future, yielding an unprecedented degree of diversity within the industry. Chapter IV will explore the differing perceptions within the industry as to the nature of the industry's problems, and the diverging business strategies that electric utilities are implementing based on their assessment of the future.

## CHAPTER II FOOTNOTES

1.  Frank W. Griffith, "The Perspective of the Chairman," Public Utilities Fortnightly, May 13, 1982, p. 23.

2.  Thomas A. Edison, as quoted by Roger W. Sant in "Coming Markets for Energy Service," Harvard Business Review, May-June 1980, p. 7.

3.  Arthur A. Thompson, "The Strategic Dilemma of Electric Utilities--Part I," Public Utilities Fortnightly, March 18, 1982, p. 19.

4.  Solar Energy Research Institute, A New Prosperity (Andover, Mass., Brick House Publishing, 1981), p. 330.

5.  The Bureau of National Affairs, Energy Users Report, Statistical Reference Files, pp. 81:0257 and 81:0261, November 1980.

6.  "Fossil Fuels Consumed by the Electric Utility Industry to Produce Electricity," Ibid, p. 81:0266.

7.  Ibid.

8.  Thompson, op. cit., p. 22.

9.  "DOE Offers a Ceiling Below Current SWU Price for Converts to US Contract," Nucleonics Week, Jan. 5, 1984, p. 1.

10. Paul Rodgers and Michael Foley, "Survey of Pending State Legislation Pertaining to Utility Regulation," National Association of Regulatory Utility Commissioners, April 7, 1983, p. 1.

11. Energy Information Administration, "Thermal-Electric Plant Construction Cost and Annual Production Expenses-1980," June 1983, EIA-0323(80), p. 8.

12. Thompson, op. cit., p. 23.

13. Charles Komanoff, Power Plant Cost Escalation (Komanoff Energy Associates, New York, N.Y., 1981), p. 22.

14. Energy Information Administration, op. cit., p. 186.

15. "Lilco Nuclear Plant Faces Possible Delay Of Over a Year, to 1986," The Wall Street Journal, Nov. 3, 1983, p. 3. See also, IRRC, "Long Island Lighting Co.," 1982 Analysis E, Supplement No. 6, p. E-76; Long Island Lighting Co., 1982 Annual Report.

16. Projection compiled by author.

17. Bureau of Economic Analysis, "Expenditures for New Plant and Equipment by U.S. Nonfarm Business in Current and Constant Dollars," Survey of Current Business, Vol. 63, No. 9, September 1983, p. 23.

18. Energy Information Administration, "Impacts of Financial Constraints on the Electric Utility Industry," EIA-0311, December 1981, p. 7.

19. Edison Electric Institute, "Financial Review 1982," August 1983, p. 11.; see also Douglas C. Bauer, "Alternative Responses to the Financial Crisis in the Electric Utility Industry," presentation to the United States National Committee of the World Energy Conference and the Edison Electric Institute, New York, N.Y., Oct. 27, 1981.

20. Energy Information Administration, "Statistics of Privately Owned Electric Utilities in the United States 1981 Annual," DOE/EIA0044(81), June 1983, p. 13.

21. Ibid., p. 16.

22. Thompson, op. cit., p. 23.

23. "Capital Appropriations," Electrical World, May 1982, p. 53; and "Capital Appropriations: A Two-Year Slide," Electrical World, June 1983, p. 43.

24. Figures for nuclear plants from Atomic Industrial Forum, "Historical Profile of U.S. Nuclear Power Development," Dec. 31, 1980, updated through October 1983. Figures for coal plants, provided by Energy Information Administration, telephone conversation, April 1982.

25. Mary C. Going, "1983 Annual Statistical Report," Electrical World, March 1983, p. 62.

26. Energy Information Administration, "Thermal-Electric Plant Construction Cost and Annual Production Expenses-1980," op. cit., p. 8.; also EIA, "Steam Electric Plant Construction Cost and Annual Production Expenses 1977," December 1978, p. XXXIII.

27. Ibid., p. 289.

28. Edison Electric Institute, "Financial Review - 1982: An Annual Report on the Investor-Owned Electric Utility Industry, July 1982, p. 8.

29. Ibid., pp. 8-9.

30. Walter G. French, "On the Attrition of Utility Earnings," Public Utilities Fortnightly, Feb. 26, 1981, p. 20.

31. Energy Information Administration, "Thermal-Electric Plant Construction Cost and Annual Production Expenses--1979," May 1982, p. 8.

32. Darrell A. Smith, "Strategic Planning: A Necessity for Utilities," Public Utilities Fortnightly, Sept. 2, 1982, p. 17.

33. John Alger, General Electric Energy Applications Program Department, telephone conversation with author, Oct. 31, 1983.

34. Peter Hunt, Peter Hunt Associates, telephone conversation with author, Nov. 17, 1983.

35. Peter Rossbach, "Conservation Efforts Shift To Gas and Elec. Projects," Energy User News, March 21, 1983, p. 1.

36. Robert H. Williams, "U.S. Energy--Out of Control," The Amicus Journal, Summer 1981, p. 12.

37. Department of Energy data as reported in Jeannie Kilmer, "Public Power Costs Less," Public Power, May-June 1983, p. 48.

38. "The Vicious Circle That Utilities Can't Seem To Break," Business Week, May 23, 1983, p. 182.

39. Energy Information Administration, "U.S.-Canadian Electricity Trade," EIA-0365, November 1982, p. 1.

40. John A. Anderson, statement at seminar on electric utility regulation, Washington, D.C., March 3, 1983.

41. Peter A. Holmes, "Pushing to Peddle Canadian Power," Fortune, Sept. 20, 1982., p. 115.

42. Energy Users Report, "New England Power Pool to Purchase Electricity From Canada's Hydro-Quebec," March 24, 1983, p. 348.

43. Business Week, op. cit., p. 189.

44. Richard Metzler, as quoted in "Remarkable Remarks," Public Utilities Fortnightly, June 9, 1983.

45. Atomic Industrial Forum, "Licensing, Design and Construction Problems: Priorities for Solution," Washington, D.C., 1978, Exhibits 1 and 9.

46. H.A. Cavanaugh, "Utility Cleaning Bill: $101 Billion by 1987," Electrical World, November 1981, p. 43.

47. Geraldine Brooks, "Dayton Power Favors Completing Zimmer As Gas-fired Unit Instead of Nuclear Site," The Wall Street Journal, Oct. 26, 1983.

48. Clyde Greenert, "The Answers to Energy Questions Lie in Politics," Energy User News, Vol. 7, No. 25, June 21, 1982, p. 34.

49. Peter Navarro, "Our Stake in the Electric Utility's Dilemma," Harvard Business Review, May-June 1982, p. 94.

50. Business Week, op. cit., p. 178.

51. Kenneth Hollister, "The Industry's Record: As Good As Its Adversaries," Public Utilities Fortnightly, Vol. 109, No. 10, May 13, 1982, p. 85.

52. Michael L. King, "Possible Change in Regulating Ohio Utilities Makes Some Analysts Nervous About Group," The Wall Street Journal, July 13, 1982.

53. "McKinney Views Preference, WPPSS, Conservation," Public Power, Sept./Oct. 1983, p. 39.

54. Michael de Courcy Hinds, "Citizen Utility Boards Hunt Industry White Elephants," The New York Times, June 6, 1982.

55. John Herbers, "Door-to-Door Lobby Effort Under Way on Energy Issues," The New York Times, March 27, 1983, p. 22.

56. Vic Reinemer, "The Other Side," Public Power, July-August 1982, p. 96.

57. David Stipp, "In Some States, Grass Roots Groups Work to Put Utility Commissioners on the Ballot," The Wall Street Journal, Sept. 29, 1982.

58. Dick Braacz, Edison Electric Institute press conference, May 27, 1983.

59. "How Institutions Voted on Shareholder Resolutions in the Proxy Season," series 1978-1983, IRRC.

60. "Utility's Shareholders Oppose Further Common Stock Dilution," News for Investors, IRRC, December 1981, p. 229.

61. "Central Maine Supports Shareholder Resolution," News for Investors, IRRC, May 1982, p. 95.

62. "Big PG&E Shareholder Sues Utility, PUC for Below-Book Sales of Stock," Electrical Week, June 21, 1982, p. 1.

63. H.A. Cavanaugh, "Can Utilities Maintain Their 'A' Rating?," Electrical World, January 1982, p. 34.

64. Irwin Stelzer and David Roe, "Viewpoint," Electrical World, May 1982, p. 59.

65. Thompson, op.cit., p. 26.

66. Dow Jones utility average, Standard & Poor's Corp., Daily Stock Price Record, 1969, Vol. IV, and 1980, Vol. I.

67. "FERC Conference Reviews Utility Financing Problems," Public Utilities Fortnightly, April 9, 1981, p. 41.

68. Herbert B. Mayo, "Inflation and Dividend Growth of Public Utilities," Public Utilities Fortnightly, March 21, 1981, p. 31.

69. Griffith, op. cit., p. 22.

70. Bauer, op. cit., Tables 2 and 6.

71. Thompson, op. cit., p. 23.

72. Figures are from EBASCO Services Inc., as quoted in Bauer, op. cit., Tables 9 and 14.

73. Edison Electric Institute, "Financial Review - 1982," op. cit., p. 7.

74. Federal Energy Regulatory Commission figures, as reported in Donald R. Gibbons, "Fuel Procurement - A Changing Responsibility," Public Utilities Fortnightly, Nov. 24, 1983, p. 26.

75. Business Week, op. cit., p. 181.

76. Hans H. Landsberg, Energy: The Next Twenty Years (Ballinger Publishers; Cambridge, Mass; 1979), p. 107.

77. Don D. Jordan, "Is America Pulling the Plug on the Future?," Public Utilities Fortnightly, Jan. 6, 1983, p. 13.

78. Robert Spann, conversation with author, July 6, 1983.

79. Planning and Forecasting Consultants Inc., press release, Aug. 24, 1982.

80. "Utilities Continue to Overstate Need for Future Power, Consulting Firm Says," Energy Users Report, May 20, 1982, p. 491.

81. Donald W. McCarthy, "The Electric Utility Executives' Forum," Public Utilities Fortnightly, June 6, 1983, p. 86.

82. Michael Foley, conversation with author, Aug. 10, 1983.

83. Lucien Smartt, "The Electric Utility Executives' Forum," Public Utilities Fortnightly, June 6, 1983, p. 78.

84. Alyssa A. Lappen, "Electric Utilities," Forbes, Jan. 5, 1981, p. 221.

85. Lelan F. Sillin, "The Electric Utility Executives' Forum," Public Utilities Fortnightly, April 9, 1981, p. 93.

# IV
# ELECTRIC UTILITY
# BUSINESS STRATEGIES
# AND THEIR RATIONALES

As the confluence of factors supporting the grow and build strategy began to unravel in the early 1970s, the reaction of the industry to its new business environment was neither swift nor sure. While certain regulatory factors and the industry's obligation to serve continued to lend some support for further growth, for many companies new economic realities more than outweighed these factors. As a result, electric utilities were suddenly faced with a number of options regarding their future business strategies. The uncertainties facing the industry were further accentuated by the fact that most utilities did not have strategic planning staffs until the late 1970s. 1/ What finally emerged was a diversity of utility strategic plans punctuated by a number of trends that were common to all of these strategies.

The diversity of strategic approaches that electric utilities are pursuing makes it difficult to categorize them into distinct groupings. Rather, the management approaches being followed by the industry now comprise a spectrum of business strategies. At one end of this spectrum are utilities that are essentially continuing to follow a grow and build strategy; at the other are utilities that have adopted a wide range of new attitudes, goals, generating technologies and financing mechanisms. The bulk of the industry is somewhere in between and appears to be muddling along and hedging its bets as to the future direction of the industry. While acknowledging the inherent difficulty of categorizing these hybrid business strategies, this chapter will discuss a number of industry trends that seem to be common to all utility business plans and then detail the major components of four discernible strategic paths that appear to be emerging among the leaders in the electric utility industry: the modified grow and build strategy, the capital minimization strategy, the renewable energy supply strategy and the diversification strategy.

Trends in the Electric Utility Industry

A number of trends are becoming increasingly common among utilities in spite of the growing divergence of their basic business strategies. The most significant of these are the use of innovative financing methods, adjustments in electricity pricing and marketing strategies and the implementation of cost reduction programs.

Innovative financing methods: As construction expenditures continued to climb while earnings lagged, many utilities have come to rely heavily on outside financing and have faced considerable difficulty in tapping traditional sources of capital. Increasingly, they are resorting to new financing techniques to fund their capital programs. Some utilities have taken advantage of recent tax law changes by selling tax benefits. Others are utilizing debt-equity swap transactions to buy back outstanding deep discount bonds and boost their common equity ratios. Still others are resorting to short-term financing for major construction projects. Philadelphia Electric, for instance, has arranged a five-year $1.1 billion revolving credit agreement to finish construction at its troubled Limerick nuclear units, although regulatory approval for the financing remains uncertain. 2/
    Among utilities with large construction programs, dividend reinvestment programs--which were given special tax considerations by Congress in 1981--have become a major source of new equity capital. Electric utilities raised more than $2 billion of new equity through these programs in 1982, about 30 percent of the $7 billion of equity financing by utilities. 3/ Some have even set up programs to sell stock to their customers through monthly installment plans.
    To supplement their domestic funding arrangements, utilities have begun to borrow funds from abroad. In the last two years, at least seven U.S. utilities have floated Eurobond issues and at least six others have negotiated syndicated bank loans outside the United States. Both types of borrowing were available in 1982 and 1983 at rates below those that utilities could have obtained In the United States.
    A number of utilities have also begun to issue bonds and preferred stock with an adjustable interest rate. With investors increasingly wary of the risks attached to the 30-year bonds that have traditionally supplied the bulk of utility debt offerings, variable rate securities offer utilities a better opportunity to sell new debt and a chance to escape current high interest rates should rates decline. For investors, they provide protection against the possibility that they will lose out if interest rates rise. Potomac Electric Power, for example, sold $50 million of flexible rate bonds in late 1981 with an interest rate that is adjusted annually to equal 116 percent of the yield on 10-year Treasury bonds.
    Another significant new financing vehicle now being used by a number of electric utilities is a type of leveraged leasing trust

arrangement to finance plant construction. Under these arrangements, tax-paying corporations, typically utility-owned leasing companies, set up a trust to buy preferred stock from a utility, using mostly borrowed capital. The corporation is able to exclude 85 percent of the dividends on the stock from taxable income, and it can deduct the interest payments on the debt. Together, the tax breaks translate into lower financing costs--1.5 percent a year for a recent 15-year deal by Pacific Gas & Electric, according to PG&E officials--and allow the utility to show less debt on its balance sheet. In the largest such arrangement so far, Dean Witter Reynolds arranged leveraged leasing in 1981 for three utilities involved in the $2 billion Colstrip coal plant in Montana. 4/

A final new financing technique is the sale of small units of common stock and bonds to ratepayers and the public. In 1980, Virginia Electric & Power (Vepco) pioneered a stock purchase plan whereby its ratepayers can purchase Vepco stock on a regular basis through added payments on their monthly utility bills. The Vepco plan has since been imitated by Montana Power, Central Hudson Gas & Electric and Puget Sound Power & Light and a number of other utilities. Meanwhile, Cleveland Electric Illuminating initiated a program in 1980 to sell small batches of its bonds to individual investors through Merrill Lynch's unit investment trust bond funds-- saving the utility millions in interest costs, according to company officials. 5/

Industry analysts expect new financing arrangements to continue to proliferate as utilities cope with changing financial markets in the coming decade. "You'll see more and more new financing mechanisms emerge that should, in aggregate, become pretty significant," predicts David V. Hedley, director of utility finance at Shearson-American Express. 6/ In the future, however, innovative financing is likely to be used increasingly as a means of avoiding high domestic interest rates rather than to gain access to funds that might otherwise be unavailable.

Changes in pricing strategies: The transition from a decreasing marginal cost to an increasing marginal cost industry has also necessitated dramatic changes in utility pricing strategies. As costs have soared, utilities have been forced to request more and larger rate increases. For utilities with major construction programs, the 5 to 10 percent yearly rate increase requests that were typical for electric utilities in the 1970s--increases that were in line with the general level of inflation--have given way to 10 to 20 percent annual rate increase requests in recent years--well above general inflation levels. Overall, utilities have opted to push for aggressive real increases in the price of electricity, contending that electric power is selling for substantially less than its free market level. This strategy has also led to the growing importance of rate case decisions for utilities. As economist Arthur Thompson points out, this has required "new and more sophisticated efforts . . . to convince regulators to grant rate increases . . . to 'sell' the need for higher rates to the public and to cope with the politics of rate increase requests." 7/

While the overall direction of the industry's pricing strategy in recent years can be summed up as "raise the rates," an important countervailing trend is beginning to emerge as many utilities confront the reality that higher rates are affecting demand and that elements of competition are beginning to erode their monopoly status. In areas where generating capacity far exceeds demand, some utilities are beginning to offer discounts on electric power to certain classes of customers or in certain geographic areas. Consolidated Edison, for instance, is offering 12 to 32 percent discounts on electricity prices to new or expanding businesses in certain economically depressed sections of Brooklyn and the Bronx in order to encourage commercial development in those areas. "We have a very large distribution network in the South Bronx and Brooklyn that's not being used," says Orlando Tanzi of Con Ed's Bronx quality control office. "We have to do maintenance on it and it's not too cost effective to maintain equipment you're not using," Tanzi notes. 8/ Similarly, Narragansett Electric, of Providence, R.I., which had seen its industrial sales plunge 12 percent in 1982 and its reserve margin top 40 percent, announced a plan In 1982 to offer 20 percent discounts to commercial and industrial customers that increase their electricity use by more than 10 percent over 1981 levels. The utility hopes to increase its load and its revenues by attracting new businesses to its service area. Other utilities that initiated discount rate programs in 1983 include Philadelphia Electric, Detroit Edison, Consumers Power, Georgia Power, Iowa Power & Light and the Bonneville Power Administration. 9/ "As competition for jobs intensifies, state regulatory commissions will become more ready to allow utilities to offer discount rates to selected customers," predicts utility consultant Robert Spann of ICF Inc. 10/

Although utilities have thus far used discounting largely to promote commercial and industrial sales, another area that seems ripe for discounts is the wholesale market--where utilities sell power to each other. Wholesale power sales dropped dramatically at some utilities in 1982 and 1983, falling about 20 percent in 1982 at American Electric Power, for instance. 11/ As more U.S. utilities attempt to sell surplus power and as Canadian utilities attempt to expand sales of cheap new hydroelectric power to the United States, competition in the wholesale market could lead to steep discounting.

Another new pricing trend is beginning to emerge among some utilities whose customers face especially large rate increases as new plants are brought into the rate base. At a number of these utilities, managers have proposed or are contemplating plans to stretch out rate increases over a period of years rather than risk the political and economic fallout of a 30-60 percent immediate rate jump--an approach known as "trending the rate base." 12/ Long Island Lighting was the first utility to propose the use of this approach, which it hopes to use if it is allowed to bring its Shoreham nuclear plant on

line in 1985. Both Detroit Edison and Arizona Public Service have
adopted the idea and filed for rate increases that would phase in the
cost of new units in four steps.

Changes in marketing strategies: Another strategic adjustment that
virtually all electric utilities have made in recent years is a change in
the emphasis of their marketing strategies away from the indis-
criminate promotion of electricity use toward the more efficient use
of electricity. Growing customer consciousness of higher rates,
government efforts during the Ford and Carter administrations to
promote an energy conservation ethic and political pressures from
regulators and activists have compelled utility advertising campaigns
to stress using electricity wisely rather than simply advocating more
electric power use. This has been true even for many utilities with
excessive reserves of generating capacity that might be expected to
be promoting electricity as vigorously as possible. A 1982 survey of
44 electric utilities by the University of Michigan's Institute for
Social Research, for instance, found that more than three-quarters
reported no electricity promotion activities while virtually all had
some information or advertising programs related to energy conservation. 13/ And a 1983 survey of 120 electric utilities by the Investor Responsibility Research Center found that 86 of the utilities
surveyed, or nearly three-quarters of the sample, had established
"formal" conservation programs. 14/
        The change in emphasis evident among utility marketing strat-
egies does not mean that most electric utilities have wholeheartedly
embraced substantial investments in energy conservation programs.
In fact, for many utilities that have large construction programs
under way, high electricity demand growth rates will be needed to
justify the added capacity, and serious conservation programs are
viewed as threatening. "The vast majority of electric utility executives have never been enthusiastic proponents of active, aggressive
conservation; in their hearts and minds electric utility executives
have believed in the necessity of a grow and build strategy to meet
the expected growth in the use of electricity," says economist Arthur
Thompson. 15/ Rather, as Arizona Public Service Chairman Keith L.
Turley has pointed out, the political pressure of strong customer interest in conservation programs has dictated at least some effort in
this area. "It would appear that whether or not federal, state or local
regulatory requirements dictate that the utility undertake some form
of conservation effort, such an effort is expected of us by our customers," Turley states. "To ignore this expectation on the part of the
utility is sheer folly. If the utility is not particularly desirous of
seeing conservation take place upon its system, it must, nevertheless,
respond to this customer desire or face the consequences of the inevitable political result," he adds. 16/
        There are already signs that the convergence of utility market-
ing strategies around the issue of conservation may not last long. In
1983, a number of utilities reinstituted their marketing operations

and began a shift back toward the promotion of electricity use. "Interest in pure conservation programs will primarily be cosmetic and political over the next several years," states ICF's Robert Spann. "If you're looking at an industry that has 35 percent more capacity than anyone wants to use, why should they spend money to tell people to use less electricity?," Spann asks. 17/

Another element of the marketing tactics being used by many utilities is increased emphasis on load leveling and market segmentation. Increasingly, utilities are using creative rate designs to promote greater electricity use when excess generating capacity is available while promoting conservation when capacity is short. In addition, they are segmenting the electricity market by designing multiple rate structures for each customer class to take advantage of the differences among those customers. "In the past, we have been successful in achieving sales through selling, which focuses rather narrowly on the seller's needs," states James Watson, director of marketing at Ohio Edison. "In the future, I believe we will be more successful in using marketing to identify the buyer's needs, especially those that can be profitably met by the seller," he adds. 18/ William C. Hayes, editor of Electrical World, agrees, stating that utilities are left with a choice between depending on "large--and possibly self-defeating--rate increases" or the "intelligent marketing of electricity" which could "increase sales and revenues while still satisfying the conservation ethic by displacing gas and oil." 19/

Cost reduction programs: A final strategic adjustment that is now common to virtually all utilities is an increased emphasis on cost reduction programs. Although utilities are pursuing cost reduction programs and efficiency improvements on a continuing basis, aside from any strategic level considerations, these activities have taken on added importance in the last several years as utility managements and regulators have scrutinized utility financial performance. From the management side, cost reduction programs seem to be getting more attention as a logical response to slowing sales growth, the lingering impact of the 1982 recession and weak earnings prospects. From the regulatory standpoint, cost reduction programs are gaining popularity as utility commissions get better information about utility costs and potential savings through management audits and as political pressures grow to find an acceptable alternative to rate increases.

Areas singled out by utilities for cost reduction effort include fuel procurement, construction and maintenance work, work force productivity, power dispatching and administration. In the fuel procurement area, utilities are using their leverage as large purchasers to extract lower prices from fuel suppliers. Houston Lighting & Power, the nation's largest user of natural gas, is exploring purchasing gas directly from the wellhead rather than from an Exxon pipeline unit for a savings of $.75 per thousand cubic feet. 20/ Pacific Gas & Electric and Commonwealth Edison have also negotiated new terms for fuel contracts in response to regulatory orders. American Electric Power closed six of its coal mines in 1982, has partially idled several others and sold part of a coal mining subsidiary in 1983 to reduce overhead.

Another area where utilities seem to be placing increased emphasis on cost cutting is employment. Utility employees are discovering that their positions no longer carry the virtual lifetime security that they once did. Dayton Power & Light, for instance, announced in June 1982 that it would cut its work force by 600 employees, or 16 percent, by the end of 1982 as part of a cost reduction program. Illinois Power recently deferred all pay increases for salaried employees for at least six months and eliminated 121 salaried positions. Pacific Power & Light cut its work force by 400 in 1983 in order to reduce its operating expenses by $49 million. Consumers Power announced in late 1983 that it would attempt to cut its 1984 operating and construction budget by more than 10 percent through layoffs, wage freezes and program cancellations. And at American Electric Power, where 1982 earnings per share fell 14.3 percent, top officials took a 5 percent pay cut in late 1982, the company laid off 1,500 employees related to the closing of some of its coal mines, hiring has been essentially frozen, and the closing of an engineering office with 860 employees was announced. "We're tightening everything we know how to tighten," explained W.S. White Jr., AEP's chairman. "We might have to take more cost-cutting steps, too." 21/

The growing interest in cost reduction programs at utilities appears certain to continue as alternative methods of improving financial performance are exhausted or become politically unacceptable. Cost reduction programs will find their way onto the agendas of all utilities, regardless of the strategic path the utility is following. However, cost cutting is not likely to become a central element of utility strategic planning. As one utility consultant notes, "operating improvements cannot resolve the corporate strategy dilemma of the electric utilities; the increasing cost economics now pervading the industry are well beyond the reach of a 'save our way to success' strategy." 22/

## Modified Grow and Build Strategy

The dramatic changes in the electric utility business environment during the 1970s have had relatively little impact on the basic business strategies of some electric utilities. These utilities are continuing to follow a strategy based on expected growth in electricity usage and additional investment in new central-station generating and distribution facilities. Commonwealth Edison and the Tennessee Valley Authority are leading examples of companies that have continued to stress new plant construction and growth. Notably, both companies have a reputation for being able to build power plants quickly and relatively cheaply.

Commonwealth Edison has seen its electricity sales drop in each of the last few years and is currently operating with a reserve margin of more than 30 percent, but nevertheless is constructing five additional large nuclear units that it expects to bring on line by 1988. The company is also retaining an order placed in 1978 for two more nuclear units--the last ordered anywhere in the United States--although it has deferred construction on these units indefinitely. Commonwealth Edison's R&D programs are average in comparison with other utilities of its size and are heavily slanted toward nuclear technology. The company is putting very little money into programs aimed at developing alternative energy sources or helping customers to conserve. The company's ambitious construction program, budgeted at $5.5 billion for the period 1983-87, is necessitating large rate increases--$503.6 million (14.8 percent) in 1981 and $660.7 million (16.7 percent) in 1982. In October 1983, the company asked the Illinois Commerce Commission for a two-step rate increase totaling $964.3 million to cover the start-up costs of two of its new nuclear units. The rate increases are attracting considerable opposition from area consumer and environmental groups. But company officials remain convinced that their strategy will pay off in the long run in the form of stable generating costs and plentiful supplies. "The construction program is putting an enormous drain and strain on the company's financial health," acknowledges James O'Connor, Edison's chairman, but "canceling doesn't make sense with the kind of investment we've made already." 23/ Whether the company will be able to continue building so many generating units at once, though, remains an open question. There are already indications that the company may have to back off from its fast track construction schedule to maintain quality control. In January 1984, a Nuclear Regulatory Commission Atomic Safety and Licensing Board denied the company an operating license for its nearly completed Byron 1 nuclear unit, citing faulty quality assurance procedures. Commonwealth Edison subsequently announced that it would have to do remedial structural work and make design changes leading to delays and an additional $900 million in construction costs. 24/

The Tennessee Valley Authority, while a leader in various experiments with utility conservation programs, also appears to be moving back toward a growth-oriented strategy.

Even utilities that are continuing to pursue a grow and build strategy, however, have recognized the need to alter parts of their past approaches and have instituted certain strategic modifications designed to counter the problems created by the new business and political environment. These modifications typically are being made in four areas--public relations efforts, plant construction scheduling, wholesale power sales and a shift away from nuclear to coal-based technologies.

Changes in public relations efforts: Utilities that are pursuing a modified grow and build strategy have made major changes in the focus and intensity of their public relations efforts. Electric utilities in general are beginning to take an active role in the energy debate and are greatly expanding their efforts to communicate their views to customers, investors, employees, regulators and the news media. This has been especially true of growth-oriented utilities, however, because of their need for large rate increases to support construction programs and because of the political opposition that such programs attract today. Sherwood H. Smith Jr., chairman and president of Carolina Power & Light, sees an expanded public relations effort as crucial to the industry's future. "For electric utilities to be successful in the years ahead we must adopt an active role in the energy debate and communicate effectively with our many publics," Smith says. "We must seek to improve the negative public perceptions of our industry. Too many persons believe that electric rates are already higher than they should be, that neither nuclear nor coal-fired generation is acceptable, that no more power plants are needed, and that the industry is insensitive to their concerns." 25/

A number of utilities have undertaken substantial advertising campaigns aimed at explaining the need for rate increases and polishing their corporate images. Long Island Lighting, for instance, is reported to have spent $800,000 in 1982 on radio advertisements designed to explain its rates and personalize its image. 26/ Meanwhile, Houston Lighting & Power has launched a major media campaign to answer questions and quell consumer complaints about rising electric rates. 27/ Many other utilities are hiring consulting economists to testify on behalf of rate increase proposals, undertake studies supporting their use of large nuclear and coal-fired generating plants, and lobby for legislative changes. Detroit Edison and Consumers Power spent more than $5 million in an unsuccessful attempt to defeat three November 1982 referenda in Michigan limiting the use of fuel adjustment clauses. 28/

Much of the industry's lobbying and public relations effort is being carried out by trade associations. In November 1981, the Edison Electric Institute--the trade association of the investor-owned segment of the industry--launched a 14-month, $2.8 million advertising campaign designed to convince the public that the industry was in financial straits because of shortsighted regulatory policies and that, in the absence of significant rate relief, electricity shortages and blackouts were likely later in the 1980s. In addition to ads in major newspapers and magazines, the campaign featured an array of public relations activities that included speeches by utility spokesmen and appearances by utility officials on television talk shows. More recently, in March 1983 a group of nuclear utilities and manufacturers launched a $30 million advertising and lobbying campaign designed to counter negative news coverage of nuclear plant cancellations, reactor accidents and cost overruns. "General public acceptance of nuclear energy has gone down in the past year and a half, and we feel what we have to do is reverse that trend," says Patrick Wheeler of the Committee for Energy Awareness, which is coordinating the nuclear companies' ad campaign. 29/

Changes in construction schedules: Another tactic that utilities pursuing a grow and build strategy are adopting is the voluntary stretching out of plant construction schedules. As utility demand growth projections have receded year by year, many utilities have delayed or deferred generating units under construction in order to avoid canceling projects outright, to ease financing burdens temporarily and to counter charges of overbuilding. Increasingly, large coal and nuclear generating projects started during the 1970s are being "mothballed" or "deferred indefinitely" by utilities counting on a resurgence in demand growth. The Tennessee Valley Authority, for instance, is maintaining four nuclear units in a deferred status at a cost of $80 million a year. TVA says that it must keep open the option of building these units in case its demand growth picks up later in the 1980s, even though its demand growth has averaged less than 1 percent per year since 1973. As of January 1984, there were 14 large nuclear reactors on order or under construction with indefinite deferral status. Virtually all of these units were owned by utilities that experienced lower than expected demand growth throughout the 1970s but that are projecting some upturn in demand growth in the 1980s.

Power sales to other utilities: Another element of the grow and build strategy is likely to be the aggressive pursuit of wholesale power sales to other utilities. In recent years, a number of electric utilities with low-cost generating capacity, including American Electric Power and the Canadian provincial utilities, have continued to build generating capacity based largely on the expectation of selling the power to other utilities outside of their service territories. In late 1983, TVA put forth proposals to market its current and expected future power surpluses to utilities throughout the South, sparking what may become a much more competitive battle for wholesale power contracts. The proposals have already engendered a considerable firestorm from some investor-owned utilities that fear competition with an expansion-minded government utility. "Some of our member companies are going to war over this," notes Fred Webber, the Edison Electric Institute's vice president for government affairs. 30/

Shift from nuclear to advanced coal and gas technologies: A final element of the grow and build strategy that is emerging from utilities' long-range plans is a continuing shift away from future nuclear plant construction toward both conventional and advanced coal technologies and gas-fired combined cycle units. Assessments of nuclear power's role in meeting future electricity demand have fallen dramatically in recent years, and further downward revisions are likely. While there were still 64 large nuclear units under construction or on order as of November 1983, virtually all of these units were ordered before 1975 and almost one-third of them appear ripe for cancellation. 31/ Few utilities are planning for any nuclear capacity growth beyond 1990 in spite of a federal energy policy favoring nuclear generation.

In contrast, a number of utilities are undertaking extensive programs to convert existing oil- and gas-fired facilities to coal and to develop advanced technologies such as fluidized bed combustion, gas-fired combined cycle units and combined cycle coal gasification. Recent surveys indicate that some utilities may have as much as 5,000 megawatts of installed capacity of advanced coal-based systems by the year 2000. 32/ Public Service of New Mexico, for instance, which expects nearly to double its installed capacity between now and the year 2000, is planning for advanced coal technologies to supply virtually all of its new capacity, with coal gasification and fluidized-bed combustion each supplying from 500 to 1,000 megawatts. 33/ Meanwhile a number of utilities are exploring gas-fired combined cycle units. "Gas-fired combined cycle plants are modular, can be added in 100 megawatt units as needed, and will have total busbar costs similar to base-load coal plants if oil stays at $30 per barrel," notes utility consultant Robert Spann. 34/

Rationale: Utilities pursuing a strategic path based on expected electricity demand growth and new power plant construction offer several rationales for adopting this strategy. First and foremost, these utilities have a passionate conviction that electricity demand growth will recover from the anemic levels of recent years to a rate closer to the annual growth that prevailed in the past. Moreover, they reject arguments made by environmentalists and some utilities that conservation and renewable energy technologies will be able to handle any increases in demand. "Conservation simply does not have the prospect for offsetting future growth," says James O'Connor, chairman of Commonwealth Edison. "Some of us in our industry have developed a don't-build-at-any-cost attitude," he adds. 35/ A. David Rossin, formerly a system nuclear engineer with Commonwealth Edison, agrees. "Amory Lovins laughs all the way to the bank as he tells people . . . that nuclear power is a dead issue," Rossin writes. "But it is the public, the individual consumer, the poorer people especially, who suffer the penalty because of the success of the activists." 36/

Many utilities see a prolonged economic recovery as the catalyst that will ignite this expected rebound in electricity demand growth. According to Marshall McDonald, chairman of Florida Power & Light, while the recent drop in electricity demand growth "provides a welcome easing of the pressures on the industry to raise capital, we do not foresee a permanent flattening of the growth rate." 37/ Similarly, Robert M. Bigwood, president of Otter Tail Power, asserts that while conservation may result in short-term changes in utility energy sales and load profiles, "it is also my conviction that economic recovery in our nation will see electric usage again rise and a more traditional usage pattern resume." 38/

The notion that a prolonged economic recovery will lead to a significant jump in electricity consumption is practically scripture to some of the industry. Indeed, the Edison Electric Institute predicts that when an economic recovery occurs, electricity demand growth will surge to such an extent that utilities will be unable to meet demand later in the decade. "We agree with the assumptions that there will be brownouts and blackouts in the near future if there is even a modest economic upturn," states EEI senior vice president, Douglas C. Bauer. 39/ Nor is such sentiment confined to certain segments of the electric utility industry. According to researcher Peter Navarro of Harvard University's Energy and Environmental Policy Center, "to meet the projected demand for electricity over the next decade, even taking energy conservation into account, utility executives would have to spend more than $300 billion for new power plants just to keep the lights on and the economy growing." 40/

A corollary argument advanced by utilities pursuing new plant construction is that new large central-station units, while expensive initially, remain the best alternative for minimizing the cost of electric power on a long-run basis. This argument is based on the belief that the price impacts of "overbuilding" are minor compared with the price impacts of continuing to burn oil and gas in baseload units. According to Navarro, "a refusal to invest will inevitably raise tomorrow's electricity rates, maintain or increase dependence on OPEC oil, and enhance the probability of blackouts or brownouts." 41/ The Department of Energy's Office of Policy, Planning and Analysis echoes the same theme in a major policy study published in 1983. According to the DOE study, "there remains a substantial economic benefit from displacing oil or natural gas as a baseload generation fuel with either new coal-fired or nuclear facilities" even under the scenario of only modest real increases in world oil prices over the next two decades. 42/

Utilities operating under a grow and build scenario also cite changes in the nature of U.S. industrial growth in support of their position. Ample supplies of electricity, they argue, are the engine that will propel economic growth, new jobs and increased productivity. Moreover, they say that the kinds of industries that are most likely to prosper in the future—the high-technology industries—are all heavily dependent on reliable electric power. "A healthy economy and a healthy supply of electricity have long been inextricably linked in the U.S.," says EEI Chairman Don Jordan. "As global competition intensifies and technology continues to drive what might be called the productivity revolution, this electrical connection will become nothing less than a lifeline. In short, electric utility capacity is the locomotive of the American economy," Jordan says. 43/ Harvard researcher Peter Navarro agrees:

Successful modernization of the American steel industry, for example, depends on the electric-arc furnace, which greatly reduces ore-handling costs, economizes on coal resources, and provides a more precise method of metal fabrication. The renaissance of the auto industry rests in large part on time- and labor-saving devices like robots, which feed greedily on electricity. The bulk of energy-saving and productivity enhancing technologies--computers, telecommunications systems, and word-processing equipment--are electricity intensive. 44/

Thus, in the view of these analysts and utility officials, electricity usage is destined to grow much faster than the economy as a whole as electricity-intensive industries grab a larger share of economic activity.

Another rationale for continuing to build large power plants--although largely unspoken by utility executives--is jobs. Large nuclear and fossil-fueled construction projects employ thousands of highly paid workers. This element appears to have been particularly important in the case of government-owned utilities like the Tennessee Valley Authority and the Bonneville Power Administration, where elected officials from the regions where these utilities operate are reported to have exerted intense pressure to keep massive construction projects going in order to preserve the jobs of thousands of unionized construction workers.

A final rationale of utilities pushing large power plant construction programs is the expectation of eventual improvements in the regulatory environment. As these utilities see it, poor regulation is the principal source of the industry's problems. "Responsibility for the mess lies primarily with the industry's regulators, who as a rule have been unable to cope with the political pressures of their job, and secondarily with the overly elaborate regulatory apparatus they have built, which, like a broken-down Rube Goldberg machine, has been unable to keep pace with post-1973 inflation," writes Navarro, summing up the feelings of many utility executives. 45/ Because the Reagan administration largely shares this perspective, some utility executives believe that regulatory reforms, in some form, are inevitable and will eventually help reduce the financial pressures on the industry, allowing it to resume its mission of providing new energy supplies.


## Capital Minimization Strategy

While many utilities have been reluctant to alter their basic business strategies, others have reacted by adopting strategies based on minimizing current capital expenditures. This strategy is especially appealing to utilities in areas of the country where there is excess generating capacity and demand growth is slowing, such as New England and the Midwest. For many of these companies, the financial uncertainties facing the industry appear to be the primary impediment to new plant construction. "The pace of capacity additions is no longer a matter of whether projected demand requires that new capacity," says a recent Electrical World forecast. "A rapidly growing number of utilities are planning new units only within their projected capacity to finance them." 46/ For a number of other utilities, however, the capital minimization strategy appears to reflect a questioning of the fundamental desirability of growth and investment. "Many executives have come to question the wisdom of making further large capital expenditures in the electric utility business," note the authors of a study conducted by Theodore Barry and Associates. 47/

Consolidated Edison of New York is a leading electric utility that is following a capital minimization strategy. The company estimates that there will be little, if any, increase in electricity sales or peak demand in its service area through the 1980s. With a reserve margin of nearly 50 percent, the company is not planning to begin construction of any new base-load capacity until the early 1990s. Because nearly 85 percent of Con Ed's generating capacity is oil-fired, however, the company hopes to convert several of its oil burning units to coal and to continue buying cheap hydroelectric and coal-fired power from other utilities. Con Ed is doing some research into alternative sources of electricity generation such as the fuel cell, but its R&D expenditures--$20.5 million in 1981 and 1982--remain modest in comparison with some other large utilities. 48/

Con Ed's cautious approach really dates back to 1974, when the company experienced such a severe financial squeeze that it was forced to omit its dividend. Since that time, the company has scrupulously avoided expensive new construction projects. In 1975, the utility also sold a nuclear plant it was constructing to the Power Authority of the State of New York. Aided by a series of rate increases capped by a $512 million (16 percent) increase in 1981 and its policy of minimizing capital expenditures, Con Ed is now praised by financial analysts as one of the strongest companies in the industry. Con Ed's common equity ratio of 50.9 percent is so high that it is drawing criticism from state legislators and the company is now taking steps to enable it to purchase up to $250 million of its outstanding common stock in order to reduce its common equity ratio.

Con Ed's future is not without its own set of challenges, of course. With rates that are easily the highest in the country and soaring profits, the company's request in 1982 for an additional $475 million annual rate increase drew sharp criticism from state officials and consumers. Moreover, the company appears to face the prospect of a gradual exodus of some of its largest customers as they leave New York City for less expensive cities or turn to alternative methods of power generation to escape Con Ed's rates. Finally, the company faces continuing uncertainties about the status of its Indian Point nuclear plant which, because of its proximity to New York City, may be shut down long before its estimated operating life of 30 years.

Utilities pursuing a strategy based on minimizing current capital expenditures--for whatever reason--are focusing on several tactics to accomplish this goal, including cutbacks in construction spending, the sale of existing generating capacity, extending plant life, demand management techniques, joint ownership of new generating facilities and power purchases.

Cutbacks in construction: One of the most widely adopted changes in policy within the industry in recent years has been the cutting back of power plant construction programs. Many utilities have discovered that, in the words of one industry observer, "less is now more" when it comes to the relationship between plant construction and utility earnings growth. In the last five years, about 140 major generating units representing more than 150,000 megawatts of capacity have been canceled or deferred indefinitely. 49/ In addition to the cancellation of units already on order, the effort by many utilities to reduce their construction programs is reflected in the dearth of new plant orders in recent years. No new nuclear units have been ordered since 1978. Moreover, during 1982 and 1983, no new orders for any major generating units were placed by utilities.

Experts predict that further cancellations--especially of nuclear units on which construction is not far advanced--can be expected during the next several years and that new orders will remain scarce. According to Electrical World's 1983 annual industry forecast, the period from 1987 to 1992 "will see what a few years ago would have been viewed as an incredibly small annual MW addition, as utilities bring on line only the last of the units already under construction." 50/ Reflecting these cutbacks, electrical utility authorizations for plans to spend funds for future construction have fallen considerably in recent years. "We could see some new coal plants started if we appear to be on a long-term growth trend again," says Douglas Bauer, senior vice president of the Edison Electric Institute, "otherwise we could go to 1990 with no new large plants ordered." 51/

Sale of existing plants: A second tactic that is in widespread use by utilities trying to reduce their level of capital spending is the selling off of portions of existing plants or plants under construction. This option is especially attractive to companies with plants in advanced stages of construction that have experienced less demand growth than expected. One characteristic of most of these sales is that they involve the investor-owned segment of the industry selling to publicly owned utilities, which often have access to lower-cost capital than do private utilities. In the last four years alone: (1) Duke Power sold most of its two-unit Catawba nuclear plant to various municipal power authorities in North and South Carolina; (2) Arkansas Power & Light sold a 40 percent interest in three coal-fired units to the Arkansas Electric Cooperative Corp.; (3) Public Service of New Hampshire sold substantial portions of its Seabrook nuclear plant to various municipalities in New England; (4) Gulf State Utilities sold a substantial percentage of its River Bend nuclear unit 1 and a coal-fired unit to various municipalities and power cooperatives in Louisiana and Texas; (5) Utah Power & Light sold substantial portions of its Hunter coal-fired plant to a cooperative and a city in Utah; (6)

Public Service Co. of New Mexico sold 29 percent of a coal-fired unit to the MSR Public Power Agency; (7) Florida Power & Light sold part of its St. Lucie #2 nuclear unit to the Florida Power Agency; and (8) Virginia Electric & Power sold 11.6 percent of its two North Anna nuclear units to the Old Dominion Electric Cooperative. 52/

Many utility industry observers expect this trend to continue, although it is likely to become more difficult to sell portions of plants that are experiencing substantial cost overruns. John Thornton, senior executive vice president of Consolidated Edison, says that "we will see further proliferation of joint public and investor-owned projects which will take various different forms . . . ." 53/ Carolina Power & Light, Duke Power, Kansas Gas & Electric, Kansas City Power & Light, Northeast Utilities, Central Maine Power, South Carolina Electric & Gas and Public Service of New Hampshire are among utilities currently attempting to sell portions of generating units.

Uprating and upgrading existing units: Another tactical adjustment being made by many utilities is to attempt to make existing generating units more productive by uprating or upgrading them. Utility spending on these activities reached $7.8 billion in 1980 and has been growing steadily since then. 54/ Uprating refers to modifications made to increase a unit's capacity. The advantages of uprating instead of building new capacity include lower capital costs and a shorter construction period. According to Anthony Bavington, power technology manager for the construction engineering firm Burns and Roe, the majority of upratings cost less than $500 per kW and can be accomplished within two to three years, whereas new fossil units could take seven to 10 years to build and are projected to cost at least 1,300 per kW. 55/

Upgrading refers to the rehabilitation of older units to extend their useful life and improve their availability and efficiency. Pennsylvania Power & Light, for example, recently asked Westinghouse to undertake a feasibility study of how to keep its 23 year old Brunner Island unit 1 operating for another 27 years. "More utilities are likely to refurbish old plants which have low embedded costs, and find ways of utilizing waste heat from power plants," says Alex Radin, director of the American Public Power Association. 56/ "Where utilities have traditionally retired power plants after 35-40 years, they now apparently intend to operate many units to 50--or even 60--years of service," adds D.S. Jenis, manager of General Electric's large steam turbine-generator marketing operations. 57/

Demand management techniques: As the costs associated with power plant construction have risen, many utilities concerned with reducing their capital expenditures have found it in their best interests to help their customers hold down peak demand by promoting various demand management techniques. "Flexibility more than cost minimization is the key to utility supply planning and more and more utilities are coming around to this view," says Alan Miller, staff attorney with the Natural Resources Defense Council. "Perhaps the biggest change is the explicit recognition that utilities can and should shape demand rather than simply prepare to respond to it," says Miller. 58/

Most utilities have instituted energy audit programs designed to aid residential customers in identifying ways to reduce energy demand. Although many utilities initiated these programs only after they were required to by the Public Utilities Regulatory Act of 1978, some established them long before regulatory fiat required it. Pacific Gas & Electric (PG&E), a leader in this area, expects to have reached half of its customers by 1990. Energy audit programs for commercial and industrial customers are also common and one utility, Seattle City Light, has gone so far as to require that certain conservation standards be met before it will allow new hookups or expanded service in commercial buildings. 59/

Many utilities have installed load management systems aimed at shaving peak load demand, especially for large industrial customers. Duke Power, for instance, says it has implemented 40 programs to reduce peak demand, resulting in documented reductions of 774 megawatts for its summer peak and about 1,600 megawatts for its winter peak. 60/ Other utilities are offering low or zero interest loans to customers who insulate, purchase heat pumps or solar water heaters, or install other energy-saving equipment. By February 1982, the Tennessee Valley Authority had lent about $185 million at zero interest to insulate one-tenth of the homes in its service area, while PG&E had $65 million of zero interest loans outstanding at the end of 1982. 61/ According to TVA, "the reduction in electric use by participants in this program will permit savings in capacity and fuel costs, thereby benefiting all consumers of TVA power through lower rates than would otherwise be required." The utility will achieve an estimated reduction in peak demand of 1,099 megawatts after an eight-year period, TVA says, "which will result in lower capacity requirements and lower generation and purchased power cost for peaking." 62/

A few utilities--including Southern California Edison, Pacific Gas & Electric, and the Bonneville Power Administration--have gone beyond loan programs to offer cash rebates or energy credits to customers who purchase energy-efficient appliances.

Overall, the impact of utility conservation and load management programs is becoming quite significant. A 1983 IRRC survey of 120 public and private electric utilities found that 54 utilities expect to reduce their peak load needs by a total of 30,633 megawatts over the next decade as a result of these programs--resulting in construction savings of $19 to $45 billion. 63/ A summary of the utilities expecting the largest peak load growth reductions from these programs is contained in Appendix C.

Joint ownership agreements: Another area to which utilities that are attempting to minimize their capital expenditures are devoting increased attention is consolidation within the industry. This consolidation is occurring principally in the form of regional or joint ownership of generating plants and equipment rather than through outright corporate mergers. Very few major electric utility mergers or acquisitions have occurred during the last 10 years, but between 1975 and 1981 the percentage of jointly owned generating capacity grew from 6.3 percent to 9.9 percent. This trend is likely to continue as utilities facing financial difficulties sell portions of plants under construction and as utilities with adjacent service areas pool their resources to construct new plants.

As is the case with the sale of existing plants, much of the increased activity involving joint ownership agreements will involve publicly owned utility systems. More than half of the nation's 2,200 public power systems are involved in such agreements today, and experts see continued growth in the number of these arrangements because of their benefits in lowering financing costs, reducing risk and allowing small utilities to take advantages of economies of scale. 64/ Forbes magazine has described the motivation for these joint ventures this way: "Clobbered by unreasonable rate commissions, fanatical environmentalists, and murderous interest rates, many utilities have stopped fighting public power and have joined it." 65/

In addition to this growth in the percentage of jointly owned facilities, the 1980s are likely to see the formation of more regional generation and distribution pools. In a number of areas, regional power pools are already responsible for dispatching generating units and routing power distribution. In a few areas, regional organizations actually own and operate generating units. Although many of these organizations consist solely of investor-owned utilities, the role of public power agencies has expanded significantly in this area as well. The Pacific Northwest Electric Power Planning and Conservation Act of 1980 (PL 96-501), for instance, effectively gives the Bonneville Power Administration the chief role in planning and financing new power plants in the Northwest. Many industry observers expect this trend toward regional consolidation to continue, and some contend that large regional "generating parks"--owned either by the federal government or by regional public utility corporations--are an absolute prerequisite if there is to be any chance of reviving the nuclear option in the United States. Interestingly, the concept of "regionalization" of the industry has garnered considerable support from Reagan administration officials as the key regulatory reform needed to break through regulatory logjams at the state level.

Purchased power: A final tactic that appears to fit in well with utilities attempting to minimize capital expenditures is increased reliance on long-term power purchase agreements and third-party developers as an alternative to new plant construction. As noted earlier, electric utilities in New England and New York are increasingly looking toward hydroelectric imports from Quebec to satisfy their future power needs. The same is true in the upper Midwest--

where eight midwestern utilities completed a study in 1983 that determined that hydropower from Manitoba Hydro would be less costly in the long run than power from new domestic coal plants--and in the West--where utilities in California are anxious to gain access to surplus power from British Columbia Hydro. "EHV [extra high voltage] transmission facilities have really become an alternative to new base-load capacity," notes Tom Watson, an attorney with Crowell & Moring. "The reason, of course, is that it is cheaper--about 50 percent of the cost of new generating capacity," Watson says. 66/

In addition to signing up for surplus Canadian power, a number of utilities are actively pursuing power purchases from industrial cogenerators and other small power producers as a means of offsetting future capacity needs. An IRRC survey of such utility power purchases identified 55 utilities, or about 46 percent of those surveyed, that are currently buying power from third-party producers--with the purchases amounting to 3,508 megawatts of capacity altogether. Moreover, projections by the utilities responding to the survey found that the amount of third-party power purchases was expected nearly to quadruple over the next 10 years, to 12,547 megawatts. 67/ Houston Lighting & Power was identified as having the largest commitment in this area, with third-party power purchases of 1,000 MW in 1982 and plans to sign up an additional 1,400 megawatts by 1992. Southern California Edison is projecting that outside entrepreneurs will develop all of the 94 MW of biomass capacity the utility plans to use by 1992, 169 of the 199 MW of wind capacity, 138 of the 259 MW of geothermal capacity and 69 of the 157 MW of solar thermal capacity. 68/ The leading utilities involved in third-party power purchases are identified in Appendix D.

Finally, third-party sales of power to non-utility customers may also become in important factor in reducing the need for new utility construction. There are a number of reasons to believe that these types of arrangements between third-party producers and energy consumers may expand even faster than many recent estimates. For one thing, the regulatory uncertainties associated with the Public Utility Regulatory Policies Act (PURPA) have been substantially reduced through recent court decisions. In addition, rapidly growing interest in the purchase of energy from small third-party producers among the U.S. military and other government agencies could indicate that such arrangements are poised for dramatic growth. "Government is displaying a heightened interest in the third-party financing arrangements that, if successful, will open the floodgates for private industry use," says Martin Klepper, a tax attorney with Lane & Edson. 69/ The recent formation of a joint venture by Wheelabrator-Frye and Garrett Corp. to build, own and operate power plants ranging in size from 3 mw to 50 mw is a further indication of the growing market for conventional plants owned by third parties.

Rationale: Utilities offer a variety of reasons for pursuing a strategy of capital minimization. For some, the decision appears to have been made by default--because any other course could have jeopardized the company's existence. One obvious example is General Public Utilities, which has clearly been forced to chart a future based on minimizing future capital expenditures since the 1979 accident at its Three Mile Island nuclear plant. The company states that its strategy is to "hold down load growth, minimize new capital investments and achieve early regulatory participation in any new projects required." 70/ Conservation and load management programs figure prominently in GPU's plans to reduce capital spending and hold down demand growth.

Financial considerations have also forced a number of much stronger utilities to adopt a capital minimization strategy. Duke Power, for instance, has acknowledged that a major change in its corporate strategy in recent years was born of necessity. The company has instituted the industry's most aggressive load management program, canceled five nuclear units and sold almost all of the capacity from two additional nuclear units. "The day existed when we wouldn't have done this on principle," says Duke Chairman Carl Horn Jr. "But when survival becomes the issue, philosophy goes out the window." 71/ A number of other utilities may soon be forced to embark on forced "capital minimization" as the result of write-offs resulting from abandoned nuclear units.

In addition to those utilities that are minimizing capital expenditures to ensure survival, a number of others view the capital minimization strategy as the logical response to their current regulatory or operating environments. "For the foreseeable future, strategies to assist the conservation of energy, reduce demand, and avoid or defer the addition of new generating capacity should be a part of the planning of all electric utilities," says W. Reid Thompson, chairman of Potomac Electric Power. 72/ In fact, some analysts argue that in view of current uncertainties a policy of husbanding corporate resources and then basically sitting on them until the smoke clears about the industry's future is the smartest strategy. Such a course, they note, ensures the utility's short-term financial integrity while allowing it to benefit from the research and experience of utilities following more aggressive strategies. Moreover, it offers the utility a better prospect of diversifying out of the utility business--should it become clear that the industry's future is less than rosy--than if a major capital program were under way. Although few utility executives are prepared to talk about that possibility, a number of industry observers are less hesitant to express their pessimism. "This industry is already slipping into a fiscal free fall" that is likely to lead to widespread bankruptcies in the absence of government bailouts, says energy consultant Peter Hunt. 73/ "Nobody ever thought a municipality could go bankrupt until it happened to Cleveland," adds Paul Bjorn, a utility expert with Price Waterhouse & Co., but now it is "an increasing possibility." 74/

Whether utilities are following a capital minimization strategy primarily in response to regulatory factors or to economic factors remains the subject of an intense debate. Many utility executives and Department of Energy officials contend that utilities are minimizing capital expenditures almost solely in response to their adverse regulatory climate--to the long-term detriment of electricity consumers. Harvard researcher Peter Navarro calls minimization of capital spending "a second-best means for a utility to meet its charter while ensuring its own survival. It is a rational response, not to the new economics of petroleum displacement, but to its own regulatory environment--of which, increasingly, it has become a financial hostage." 75/ Other analysts, however, view the capital minimization strategy as rational not only from a regulatory standpoint but from a broader economic standpoint as well. "It may well turn out that for this period a capital minimization strategy is the correct stance for regulator, utility and consumer alike," says Douglas Jones, director of the National Regulatory Research Institute. "Surely this is so at the micro level, where utilities have overcapacity, unusually high reserve margins, and stagnant or declining service territories," Jones adds. 76/ A similar view is espoused by Andrew Reynolds of the Energy Information Administration, who says that "we could view capital minimization as a strategy of regulation avoidance and asset maximization--that is, economic use of investment capital, efficient use of existing generating resources, sharing surplus capacity through joint ownership and power transfers, promoting conservation, and searching the market place for investments in energy supplies that are unbridled by regulation." 77/

A final reason why some utilities are minimizing their capital expenditures is that, for many of them, it is in the best interests of their shareholders. "Utilities that still consider new plant construction as a financial opportunity, instead of a necessary evil, have not yet learned a very expensive lesson," warn utility consultant Irwin Stelzer and environmentalist David Roe. 78/ Soaring construction costs coupled with low stock prices have virtually guaranteed that utilities engaged in ambitious construction programs in recent years have diluted their stockholders' equity. According to utility investor William Kessler, dilution during the 1970s reduced the book value of Union Electric, for example, by $70 million and of The Southern Co. by $339 million. In 1980, one survey of 85 major electric utilities found that of the 57 utilities that issued new common stock that year, 56 were forced to sell it at below book value, and the average sale occurred at 70 percent of book value. For the industry as a whole, dilution of common stock book value resulting from such sales averaged about 2.9 percent in 1980. 79/

## Renewable and Alternative Energy Supply Strategy

A third major strategic option that is emerging for utilities is an emphasis on the development and use of renewable and other non-conventional energy technologies. This strategy seems most appealing to utilities with rapidly growing service territories and regulatory climates that discourage nuclear and coal plant construction. At present, only two major investor-owned electric utilities have committed themselves to this strategy, and both--Southern California Edison and Pacific Gas & Electric--are in California.

In theory, a non-conventional energy supply strategy could be seen as similar to the "grow and build" strategy described earlier except that each faces different technological challenges, cost curves and environmental problems. In practice, however, the two examples of utilities that are actively adopting a renewable technology supply strategy suggest that they are making a major break with traditional utility planning concepts. Among the most significant components of this new supply strategy--at least as it has been articulated by PG&E and SCE--are a shift toward the use of renewable resources, increased research and development efforts, and a focus on the addition of small, modular units of capacity.

Shift toward renewables: A number of utilities are exploring renewable energy sources--that is energy sources based on essentially infinite sources of energy rather than on finite fuel stocks--and many are now operating limited R&D projects. But one utility--Southern California Edison--stunned the industry in October 1980 by committing itself to a corporate strategy based on renewable resource development. In a letter to all company employees, SCE Chairman William R. Gould wrote, "It is the policy of Edison to devote our corporate resources to the accelerated development of a wide variety of future electrical power sources which are renewable rather than finite. These include wind, geothermal, solar, fuel cells, small hydroelectric, and continued emphasis on cogeneration, conservation and load management. As a result of some significant successes in a number of research and development areas," Gould continued, "we now believe that some forms of power generation which a few years ago were speculative or unproven have progressed to the point that they can be aggressively developed and relied upon to provide a significant part--perhaps about 30 percent--of the electricity to supply the additional needs of our customers later this decade." 80/ Subsequently, Southern California Edison committed itself to a goal of adding 2,150 MW of renewable and alternative generating capacity by 1992. By the end of 1982, the company had 1200 MW of alternative and renewable energy sources on line, under construction, or represented by signed contracts or letters of intent. 81/

In 1981, Pacific Gas & Electric announced that it too would concentrate on development of renewables. The company said that except for completion of its long-delayed Diablo Canyon nuclear project, it would rely entirely on geothermal power, cogeneration and renewables for its new generating needs in the 1980s. Geothermal capacity--where PG&E is already the world's leading utility with 1,000 MW on line--is expected to grow by another 700 MW and the company has plans for an additional 1,400 MW of hydroelectric capacity. 82/

The clear emphasis on <u>renewable</u> energy development by Southern California Edison and Pacific Gas & Electric appears to differentiate their strategy from either a conservation-oriented approach or a strategy based on the development of advanced nonrenewable technologies such as coal-gasification and fluidized bed combustion. Although both SCE and PG&E have extensive conservation programs, the primary direction of their strategic planning is to meet growing electricity demand through development of renewable resources, not to reduce demand as much as theoretically possible. Both utilities, in fact, expect their demand to grow by about 50 percent between now and the end of the century, requiring the addition of about 8,000 megawatts of capacity to each system. <u>83/</u> "Our previous position was that we were going to rely on conservation and supplement that with renewable and alternate sources as they came along," explains Glenn Bjorklund, Edison's vice president for system development. "Our major policy change is to make renewables our preferred technology--to make it happen." <u>84/</u> In addition, although both utilities are continuing R&D efforts related to various advanced nonrenewable generating technologies, they are giving their renewable R&D programs priority over these efforts. This stands in marked contrast to the rest of the industry, which is concentrating on advanced coal technologies to provide the bulk of its nonconventional generating capacity additions over the next two decades.

<u>Increased research and development efforts</u>: Expanded research and development efforts are another somewhat obvious element of a renewable energy supply strategy. Some of these technologies are considerably more efficient than existing generating technologies, offering the prospect of improved fuel utilization and lower costs. Such technologies will not live up to their potential, however, unless electric utilities devote greater resources toward research and development. Both Southern California Edison and Pacific Gas & Electric have significantly expanded their R&D spending in recent years, while the majority of the industry has not. For the three year period 1980-82, Edison's R&D spending totaled $151 million, or 1.3 percent of electric operating revenues, and PG&E spent $180 million, or 1.7 percent. Meanwhile, according to the Electric Power Research Institute, the electric utility industry as a whole has been investing in R&D at a rate of about 0.65 percent of revenues--far below the rate of 1.9 percent for all U.S. industry, 1.3 percent for the U.K. Central Electricity Generating Board and 2.0 percent for Electricite de France. <u>85/</u>

Increased research and development spending is likely to receive greater attention from all utilities in the 1980s in view of the potential rewards and the Reagan administration's proposals for a drastic cutback in government research on renewable and fossil fuel generating technologies. Gerald F. Tape, chairman of an EPRI advisory council, says "one is left . . . with the impression the current electric utility R&D support level is low, both when compared to

other industries and, especially, in view of the job to be done." 86/
The most ambitious R&D programs are likely to be implemented by
utilities pursuing alternative energy development, however, with an
emphasis on new technologies, load management and cogeneration.
Utilities in low-growth areas pursuing other strategies may concentrate their R&D efforts on extending the life of existing plants, improving the reliability of these facilities and exploring investment
opportunities in cost reduction programs and non-utility businesses.

Small increments of capacity: Another element of the renewable
energy strategy appears to be an emphasis on the addition of small,
modular units of capacity. The vast majority of the renewable
energy projects now on utility drawing boards involve capacity additions of less than 100 MW. In fact, most of the units currently on
line or under construction are under 10 MW in size.
     One reason for the small scale of present renewable energy
projects, of course, is that these technologies are still in the early
stages of commercialization. Equally important, however, is the fact
that many renewable technologies do not lend themselves to economies of scale. Rather, they are typically modular in nature, allowing
capacity to be installed quickly in small units as needed. Alfred
Canada, an engineer who is pushing the concept of solar photovoltaic
plants, believes, for instance, that modularity is one of the most important characteristics of such plants. "Properly engineered as a
system, modules or groups of modules can go on-line as procured and
installed," Canada writes. "Capacity at a licensed site can grow with
system demands under a single regulatory processing," he adds, reducing capital requirements and shortening licensing times. 87/
Perhaps equally important in the minds of utility planners is the fact
that small, modular projects can be canceled easily. In 1983, for instance, the California Public Utility Commission lowered PG&E's buy
back power rate by an average of about 1¢ per kWh in response to
very high levels of hydroelectric generation, immediately reducing
interest in new oil and gas-fired cogeneration projects in PG&E's
service territory. 88/

Rationale: Utilities and energy analysts give a number of reasons for
the movement toward greater use of renewables. Some analysts
claim that the particular regulatory climate in California was the
primary motivation behind the switch in strategy by SCE and PG&E.
"You look at conventional energy alternatives, at least in California,
and there aren't any alternatives," says Ronald Watkins, vice president for resource planning at San Diego Gas & Electric, another
California utility. 89/ "The regulatory process effectively prohibits
nuclear, it's extremely difficult to use coal, you can't count on using
oil, you have to phase out natural gas, all that's left is alternative
options," explains Richard Balzhiser, vice president for research at
the Electric Power Research Institute. 90/ But while no one disputes
that California's regulators have made it difficult to site and con-

struct new nuclear and coal projects, SCE and PG&E officials do not
agree that their new corporate objectives were dictated primarily by
regulators. "Our expectation is that by 1990 the electric utility
world will have grown into a mature acceptance of a broad range of
alternative resources," says Jane Bergler of PG&E's federal agency
relations department. 91/ A Southern California Edison program
director is even more direct:

> SoCal Edison has one of the best internal R&D groups in the
> utility business. Mr. Gould is one of the brightest minds in
> this business and in the whole engineering profession. We're
> leaders. We made the decision because we think it's right
> for us and that we're going to make money on it. Sure it's
> easy to second guess when you're on the outside, but this
> program wouldn't have a chance if we didn't believe in it
> ourselves. Outsiders don't run our show. 92/

Aside from the regulatory environment, one major reason for the
growing interest in renewables is that their small scale and modularity gives utilities greater flexibility and reduces financial risks. Wind
farms, solar power towers or photovoltaic plants, biomass and geothermal plants can all be built in two or three years in contrast to the
10- to 15-year lead times now typical for nuclear and coal-fired
stations. "Long lead-time, capital-intensive plants are particularly
inflexible beasts--unable to respond quickly to changes in demand,
technology and regulatory requirements," notes David Roe of the
Environmental Defense Fund's energy program. "With small pieces,
no one commitment is overwhelming, and the direction and pace of
growth can be continuously adjusted. Financially, the lower risk
translates into immediate dollar benefits for utilities and their
shareholders." 93/ Glenn Bjorklund, vice president for system development at Southern California Edison, agrees. "The age of the
dinosaur--the large, central power plant with a 10-to-15-year lead
time--may have passed," says Bjorklund. 94/
    Concerning financial risks, Alex Radin argues that "maximum
diversification appears to be the most prudent strategy for utility
power supply planning and utilization." 95/ And regarding flexibility,
Leonard Hyman, a vice president with Merrill Lynch, agrees that
when "you're dealing with smaller increments you can be more flex-
ible." In Hyman's opinion, "more utility companies will be absolutely
obliged to look at all these alternative sources." 96/
    Another reason for the shift toward renewables is that it allows
a utility to reduce financial risks further by contracting with outside
developers to build and operate small-scale plants. This option is not
available with most nuclear or coal-fired plants because of the large
scale and enormous capital investment needed to achieve economic
efficiency. Contracting effectively allows a utility to position itself
as an energy broker--shifting much of the economic risk for developing new capacity to third-party developers. The utility can con-

tinue to build plants for which there is a reasonable assurance of an acceptable return on investment, but it is not forced to provide the capital for all new generating facilities in its service territory. PG&E, for instance, pays 4.4 cents per kilowatt hour plus a capacity payment for the power it purchases from small producers--well below its own long-run marginal cost for power and the rate it charges customers. Recently, the company applied for regulatory approval to buy all of the 126 MW output from 36 huge wind generators to be built by Boeing. "We have benefits from this in the power which we will be getting and in the elimination of capital costs we would otherwise have to pay if we wanted to handle such a project ourselves," says Michael Russo of PG&E's generation planning department. 97/ As noted earlier, the use of third-party developers will not be limited to utilities using renewable resources. Nevertheless, the modular nature of many renewable energy sources suggests that utilities pursuing a renewable supply strategy are likely to make the greatest use of outside entrepreneurs.

A final rationale that some analysts are citing for a renewable energy supply strategy is the argument that since greater use of renewables is inevitable--because of the increasing cost of finding and extracting non-renewable fuels--it behooves utilities to gain as much experience with the new technologies as possible now so that they will be in the best position to capitalize on them as they become economic. Although there is a great deal of uncertainty as to the exact time when various renewable technologies will become cheaper than conventional generating systems dependent upon non-renewable fuels, few analysts doubt that this point will indeed be reached. A number of renewable technologies--including hydro, geothermal steam and wind--are already cost competitive with conventional generating systems at the margin, and other renewable technologies are expected to become competitive within the next decade. The question thus becomes one of picking the correct time to switch from the escalating cost curves associated with conventional (oil, gas, nuclear and coal-based) generating systems to the falling cost curves associated with the renewable technologies.

In the view of some analysts who advocate the renewable strategy, those utilities that make the switch first will gain a decided advantage over utilities that wait until the cost curves have actually crossed before they begin to reorient their R&D and construction programs. The utilities that switch first may be able to contract for all of the production from efficient manufacturers of some renewable systems, these analysts argue, thereby freezing out other utilities for a period of years. Meanwhile, utilities that commit themselves to new conventional generating projects will be forced to use those sources for several decades in order to recover their investments in them--even if rising fuel costs or breakthroughs in renewable technologies make them economically obsolete long before they are physically worn out. Some utility officials even argue that the lack of any major generating plant orders in 1982 stems as much from the imminent commercial status of various alternative technologies as from the well-publicized financial pressures afflicting the industry. As Arthur Thompson sums up the situation, more utilities may look toward renewables because they will have no other choice:

> The point is that it would be a gross strategic error for an electric utility to define its business as one of "supplying electricity only through the form of central-station generating technology." While utility executives may have emotional attachment to such a concept, and while investors have a huge financial stake in maintaining the virtual monopoly of this technological approach, customers are more flexible. Customers are likely to switch in droves to alternate energy sources as soon as these sources are competitive on reliability and cost.

> Hence, unless electric utilities are to forfeit their market position as the supplier of electric energy, they must look hard at diversification into alternate technologies for supplying electric energy. 98/

A growing number of utility executives are beginning to agree. According to APPA director Alex Radin, "the use of renewable energy sources has become deeply ingrained in the consciousness of the American people and public power systems would be well-advised to intensify their interest in such resources." 99/ And in the words of Jerry L. Maulden, chief executive officer of Arkansas Power & Light, "Do we simply sit back and watch conservation, cogeneration and renewable resource development remove a share of our markets or do we instead attempt to compete on an equal footing with the competition?" 100/

## Diversification Strategy

A fourth major strategic option available to electric utilities involves diversification outside of the electric power business. With returns on equity from the regulated utility business stuck near 11 percent for the last decade, many utilities began exploring the possibilities of investing in faster-growing, more profitable ventures such as oil and gas exploration, coal mining, energy and engineering services, real estate, computer services, telecommunications and fish hatcheries. "Market-to-book ratios have fallen, earnings-per-share growth has diminished, and the financial risks of generation expansion have increased. Logically, this has encouraged utility executives to consider other businesses," notes a study prepared in 1981 by Portland General Electric's corporate planning division. 101/ "For an industry that's in economic disequilibrium, diversification is about the only bright hope that I see," adds John Attalienti, utility analyst at Argus Research Corp. 102/

Figure 8.

## Utility Industry Diversification Efforts

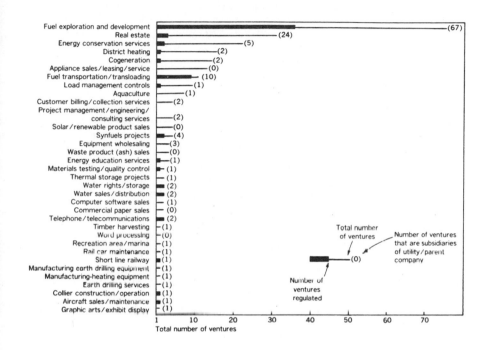

SOURCE:   Electrical World.

Scope of activities: While many electric utilities remain opposed to diversifying beyond their basic business of electric power generation, transmission and distribution, a 1982 Edison Electric Institute survey shows the extent to which the industry has begun to diversify. The EEI study found 82 of the trade association's 128 members surveyed had one or more business ventures outside of their traditional electric power business. EEI's 1981 survey--the results of which are summarized in Figure 8 and shown in detail in Appendix A--found 79 investor-owned electric utilities involved in 247 business ventures not directly related to electric power. 103/

While the number of utilities that have branched out into other businesses is clearly large and growing, only a few utilities have diversified to the extent that it is having a major impact on their bottom lines. A 1981 survey of 100 utilities by Salomon Brothers found that only six had diversification efforts that accounted for at least 10 percent of revenues. 104/ "There just isn't much to latch onto yet," when it comes to diversification efforts, adds Doris Kelley, a Merrill Lynch analyst. 105/

Types of diversification: Electric utility diversification efforts are so varied that different types of diversification plans can almost be seen as separate strategic options. In one sense, the renewable energy supply strategy discussed earlier in this chapter is a specific type of diversification strategy aimed at electricity supply technologies. In addition, electric utilities are pursuing at least four other approaches to diversification: energy-related and complementary products, energy services, nonrelated products and services, and other utility businesses. Although certain types of diversification are more common than others, there are an extremely wide range of utility investments outside of the electric power business. "I see a certain randomness in the areas chosen for diversification based on the interests of the senior executives involved," says Robert Malko, chief economist at the Wisconsin Public Service Commission and a utility diversification expert. 106/

Energy-related and complementary products--The most common type of diversification activity by electric utilities involves participation in the production and sale of products related to the energy business. At least 75 utilities are participating in fuel exploration or development efforts--by far the largest category of diversification found by the EEI survey. In many cases, these ventures are an attempt at greater vertical integration--with a fuel exploration subsidiary attempting to develop coal, oil, gas or uranium reserves that can be utilized by the parent utility. In other cases, however, utilities have formed fuel subsidiaries exclusively to market to other customers. Houston Industries, for instance, is a utility holding company with two fuel subsidiaries. Utility Fuels Inc. supplies the holding company's operating utility--Houston Lighting & Power (HL&P)-- with coal, uranium and lignite. Meanwhile, Primary Fuels Inc. explores for and develops oil and gas reserves to sell to outside customers.

The growth of utility fuel development subsidiaries in the area of coal development over the last decade has been particularly dramatic. Total coal production by the electric utility industry rose nearly six-fold between 1970 and 1980, reaching 95 million tons in 1981. During that decade, the percentage of the utility industry's coal consumption supplied by captive coal production rose from 4.8 percent to 15.8 percent. Among the electric utilities with the largest coal mining operations are Texas Utilities, Pacific Power & Light, American Electric Power and Montana Power. 107/

Utility production of other fuels is much less substantial but could grow rapidly later in the decade if utilities continue to increase their investments in exploration. New England Electric System (NEES) is a prominent example of a utility committed to oil and gas development. Since 1974, the utility has had a partnership with an

Samedan Oil Corp. to explore and develop domestic wells, and in recent years NEES has been investing in excess of $100 million annually in domestic exploration activities. The joint venture provided NEES with about 2.1 million equivalent barrels of oil and natural gas in 1983, and under a 15-year development plan announced in 1980 the utility expects to spend $100 million a year to boost its production to 7 million barrels in 1995. 108/ Other electric utilities with major oil and gas activities include Montana Power, Houston Industries and Montana-Dakota Utilities. 109/

Aside from fuels production, the major areas of interest among utilities in the energy-related products group include appliance sales, steam production, and sales of electrical and energy management equipment. Solar hot water heaters, heat pumps and cogeneration equipment are rapidly gaining popularity among utilities' sales staffs as products that can be marketed profitably--although in almost all cases utilities are not currently manufacturing their own products. In many cases, utilities have been encouraged to enter these markets by their regulators because of the belief that the private sector was not doing enough to provide energy-efficient appliances.

There also appears to be growing interest among some utilities in manufacturing energy systems. Northern States Power and Green Mountain Power have expressed interest in manufacturing power equipment for industry. And Wisconsin Power & Light recently bought Windworks Inc., a Wisconsin-based manufacturer of wind generators, for $2.5 million. "We are very excited about this," says WP&L planner Daniel Gomez-Ibanez, "not only because Windworks has good earnings potential but because ultimately, we see society as moving toward renewable, sustainable sources of energy." 110/

The sale and servicing of energy-related products by utilities may be stunted, however, by growing opposition from small business for antitrust reasons. Small businesses fear that they cannot compete with utilities in areas such as advertising, access to credit and market data, and financial resources. Such fears are already translating into heated political pressure and rhetoric. "Competition from public utility companies engaged in non-utility businesses is one of the most serious threats facing small business today," contends New Mexico state senator Thomas Lewis. 111/ Few, if any, state utility commissions are set up to handle such antitrust questions. Nevertheless, "there could be a lot of pressure on regulators to decide these anti-competitive claims," notes Charles Gray, assistant general counsel for the National Association of Regulatory Utility Commissioners (NARUC). 112/

Energy services--A second major area of diversification is the marketing of energy services. Many electric utilities are trying to capitalize on their expertise in the energy business by marketing energy audit services to customers interested in implementing energy conservation plans. Iowa Resources, for example, has formed a subsidiary called Enserco that markets an integrated energy management service to large, industrial clients for fees ranging from $500,000 to

$2.5 million. 113/ The service includes energy audits, equipment selection and purchase. According to Paul Levy, chairman of the Massachusetts Department of Public Utilities, such conservation services are "a good business opportunity" for utilities that will boost earnings. 114/

Other utilities are attempting to market technical expertise or training in areas where they have developed specialized skills. New England Electric System has licensed a utility load management system that it developed to Emerson Electric for marketing to the industry. Duke Power, which has an impressive record for designing and constructing its own generating facilities, is exploring the possibility of marketing this expertise to other utilities. Meanwhile, The Southern Co., Detroit Edison and American Electric Power have each recently formed new subsidiaries to market technical expertise in power plant design, engineering, construction planning, and operation to utilities and industrial customers.

Nonrelated products and services--A third type of diversification effort that is receiving increased interest from utilities involves diversification into areas completely unrelated (or only tangentially related) to the electric power business. The most common types of unrelated activities that utilities are pursuing include real estate development, fuel and cargo transportation and storage, timber management, fish hatcheries and financial services. Many of these nonrelated ventures appear to be accidents of history or remnants of diversification efforts dating back many years. A growing number, however, are the result of recent strategic management decisions. Many represent spinoffs from a utility's other operations--real estate and timber management from land acquired for power plant sites, barge and rail transportation systems acquired to service generating plants, and customer billing or collection services that make use of existing utility computer systems. Northeast Utilities, for example, is planning to build 800 luxury condominiums on a 42-acre site it owns in the Stamford, Conn., waterfront area. Meanwhile, as an offshoot of its hydroelectric operations, Montana Power has diversified into the computerized automation equipment business for utility and industrial applications.

One interesting spinoff business being explored by utilities is the use of waste heat for food production. A number of utilities--including San Diego Gas & Electric, Southern California Edison, Sierra Pacific Power, Wisconsin Electric, Pacific Power & Light and Long Island Lighting--have experimented with raising lobsters or fish in the warm water that results from cooling generating plants. Probably the most ambitious fish production effort, however, is being undertaken by Public Service Electric & Gas. The company is now producing about a million pounds of rainbow trout a year at its Mercer generating station and its Limestone Springs Fishing Preserve. 115/ "Once we prove this is successful, by the year 2000 the utility industry could be involved with food processing right up to its ears," predicts Bruce L. Godfriaux of PSE&G's research and development section. 116/

One other business in which some utilities seem destined to increase their involvement is financial services. A number of utilities now have extensive low-interest loan programs aimed at reducing the need for new plant construction through the financing of customer insulation and conservation programs. Although many of these programs were started because of pressure from regulatory authorities, it seems likely that some utilities will come to see financial services--especially the lending of capital to finance conservation and new energy sources--as a legitimate business opportunity. As Amory Lovins says, "utilities have three advantages in taking a sizable share of this new market: they already invest about as much money as is needed to bring the energy transition to maturity; they already have a billing relationship with nearly everyone; and they have a strong incentive not to go broke." 117/ Utilities may also come to view financing as a means of fostering their area development programs. Wisconsin Electric Power, for instance, recently announced that it wants to set up a new subsidiary to finance growing businesses in Wisconsin and help them fend off unfriendly takeover attempts by out-of-state companies.

Other utility businesses--A final avenue for electric utility diversification is the acquisition of other utility franchises. Pacific Power & Light (PP&L) is the leading example of an electric utility that has taken this approach. For a number of years the company owned a major interest in Telephone Communications Inc., a holding company for various local telephone exchanges in the Pacific Northwest. In 1979, PP&L significantly expanded its commitment to telecommunications by acquiring Alascom Inc. from RCA for $200 million. Alascom provides interstate and intrastate telecommunications, telex and telegram services within Alaska and between Alaska and the rest of the world. PP&L is continuing to invest in various businesses in the telecommunications and information service fields--although many of these investments are in unregulated areas --and its telecommunications businesses provided $344 million in revenues in 1982.

In addition to telecommunications, the most prominent areas of utility involvement in regulated businesses are oil and gas pipelines, water sales and cable television. Perhaps the most interesting option for utility expansion of regulated business stems from the exploding market potential for electronic information systems in homes and offices. Many companies, including some electric utilities, are studying the possibilities for integrated information systems that would provide services such as electronic banking and bill paying, energy system management, cable and satellite television programming and computer services. According to James Akers, the Edison Electric Institute's director of economic policy analysis, "significant synergies between electric power distribution and telecommunications are emerging with particular opportunities seen in cable television." 118/ It remains uncertain, of course, whether electric utilities will be in a position to compete effectively with other large companies eyeing this market.

Electric utility diversification into other regulated businesses may become more common as a result of the historical reluctance of non-utility companies to enter regulated businesses. With the stock prices of many utility companies selling at very small multiples of cash flow, some utilities may decide that it is an opportune time to expand through acquisitions. In 1983, Missouri Public Service Co., an electric and gas utility based in Kansas City, made a successful tender offer for Gas Service Co., a natural gas distributor in neighboring states.

Structural options for diversification: In addition to examining the economic potential of various types of businesses, utilities following a diversification strategy confront choices about the organizational structure best suited to their particular business plan. During the 1960s and 1970s, utilities diversified predominantly by creating wholly owned subsidiaries to carry out new activities. One problem with this approach, however, was that, in some states, regulators were passing on the profits from unregulated subsidiaries to utility ratepayers. "In virtually every case that I am aware of," noted Terry Ferrar, vice president of economics for the Edison Electric Institute, "transactions between unregulated, profitable subsidiaries and parent electric utilities give rise to continuing concern over . . . consolidated profitability by the commission when setting rates on the electric part of the business." 119/

Concerns such as these have prompted renewed interest in recent years in the formation of utility holding companies because of the advantages this particular organizational structure has in shielding subsidiary profits. Although most electric utilities with a single operating company have long shunned the idea of forming registered holding companies because of certain requirements under the Public Utility Holding Company Act of 1935 (PUHCA), the advantages of holding company status may now outweigh the disadvantages. A 1981 study on utility diversification by the Wisconsin Public Service Commission noted, "The holding company structure may allow the utility the greatest freedom in pursuing ventures that are not directly related to utility business and that have the potential to penetrate large markets beyond the utility. The holding company format also removes many restrictions to external financing of new ventures." 120/

At present, there are 14 registered utility holding companies-- typically those that own utilities in more than one state--that are subject to SEC regulation under PUHCA. A number of other electric utilities have formed holding companies and won exemptions from direct SEC regulation because they meet certain requirements of the 1935 act. In the 47 years since the act was passed, there have been few court challenges, leaving very unclear just how restrictive it is. Moreover, as discussed further in Chapter V, there are serious attempts under way--supported by the Reagan administration and the SEC--to weaken or abolish PUHCA. Indianapolis Power & Light,

Wisconsin Electric Power, Virginia Electric & Power, Wisconsin Power & Light, and Baltimore Gas & Electric have all recently announced plans to form holding companies.

If electric utilities are unable to diversify without penalizing the regulated portions of their business, some companies may adopt other tactics. One tactic that is becoming increasingly common among gas utilities is divestiture--dividing utility and non-utility businesses and spinning them off to shareholders as separate companies. One electric utility--Central Louisiana Energy--has already pursued such a course. Back in the early 1970s, the company diversified into oil and gas exploration. But aided by a large gas discovery in 1978, non-utility activities grew to account for two-thirds of operating revenues and 77 percent of profits by 1980. When the Louisiana Public Service Commission began to insist that the electric utility should share in the profits of a subsidiary that was selling gas to the utility, Central Louisiana appealed and got permission from the Louisiana Supreme Court to split up the company. In November 1981, former parent-company investors received stock in the newly independent electric utility. 121/ Although it seems unlikely that electric utility divestitures will become common, a number of companies do not rule out the idea. "If there is evidence that the success of our other businesses is having an impact on the regulators as they set our rates, it would not be in the shareholders' interest to maintain the company as a whole," says Don C. Frisbee, chairman of Pacific Power & Light. 122/

Another tactic that could become increasingly popular among utilities that are holding companies is to set up generating company subsidiaries that own power plants and sell power to operating companies of the holding company or unaffiliated utilities. The Southern Co. has done this through its SEGCO subsidiary, which owns a plant in Alabama and sells power to Alabama Power and Georgia Power--two other Southern Co. subsidiaries. American Electric Power has also set up a generating company subsidiary that will own 30 percent of a new 1,300 MW coal plant. Virginia Electric & Power applied for permission to set up a generating company in late 1983 and two senior officials at Pacific Gas & Electric have advocated the idea in a journal article.

The principal advantages of forming generating subsidiaries appear to be additional financial flexibility and the shifting of regulatory jurisdiction from the state public utility commission to FERC, a federal agency that regulates wholesale power sales. FERC is widely considered by the industry to be more responsive to utility revenue requests than are many state regulatory commissions. "Many people are looking into switching to federal regulation because they think FERC is giving away the store," says Herbert Blinder, director of technical services for the American Public Power Association. 123/ Nevertheless, utility attempts to establish generating companies remain subject to approval by state regulatory authorities.

Regulatory response to diversification: The growing interest in diversification by electric utilities has prompted some legislators and utility regulators to take steps aimed at limiting or controlling the process. Attempts by utilities to diversify "raise many legal, economic and financial issues which should be considered by state regulatory commissions," says Robert Malko of the Wisconsin Public Service Commission. 124/ Under the auspices of The National Association of Regulatory Utility Commissioners, a number of state regulators have begun to examine the issues raised by utility diversification efforts. A 1982 report issued by NARUC discussed a number of these issues and recommended procedures that regulators could follow to monitor and control diversification. Figure 9 shows the major issues raised by diversification as outlined in the NARUC report.

It remains to be seen just how active many states will be in attempting to control utility diversification efforts. In several of states, legislators and regulators have already moved strongly to head off diversification. In 1982, the New Mexico legislature voted a moratorium on utility diversification pending further study of the regulatory issues involved. And in June 1983, the Maryland Public Service Commission blocked an attempt by Baltimore Gas & Electric to form a holding company, arguing that state law prohibited the move. "As time goes by, utilities are going to have a smaller and smaller degree of freedom to diversify," contends Robert Malko. "It's not going to be that easy for them to form new holding companies." 125/ Utility diversification is proceeding in many states, however, and ultimately the issue may be decided by the courts and Congress.

Rationale: Advocates of diversification put forth a number of reasons for utilities to pursue this strategy. One major reason cited for diversifying is avoidance of regulation. According to this argument, utilities are rushing to diversify because the returns that regulators allow on the utility business are not competitive with those available on unregulated businesses and are insufficient to attract new capital. "One obvious direction for the investor-owned utility is to free itself from regulatory inequities by shifting assets to non- or near-regulated diversification," states an Edison Electric Institute paper. 126/

Some observers, however, believe that utility diversification efforts stem more from a general reaction to the underlying economic prospects for the utility industry than from adverse regulatory prospects. As Robert Malko sees it, "The inability of electric utilities to earn their allowed rate of return" has been the major factor prompting consideration of diversification, rather than the inadequacy of the allowed returns set by regulators. 127/ Clearly, some utility executives feel that it is essential to move into businesses with better long-term growth and profit potential despite the costs and risks involved in expanding into new business areas. As Pacific Power & Light Chairman Don Frisbee has noted, one factor in his

Figure 9.

## Common Issues In Utility Diversification

### Regulatory Issues

- Risk to rate-
  payers

- Adequate regu-
  latory authority

- Accounting pro-
  cedures

- Regulatory
  review

- Timing and extent
  of diversification

- Federal involve-
  ment

### Legal Issues

- Access to books,
  records and offi-
  cers

- Divestiture of
  utility

- Organizational
  structure

- Divestiture of
  diversified activ-
  ity

- Geographic loca-
  tion of diversifi-
  cation

- Diversification
  into other regu-
  lated industries

### Economic Issues

- Allocating
  common costs

- Relationship to
  utility activities

- Transfer pricing

- Rate of return dif-
  ferences: utility
  vs. non-utility

- Utility manage-
  ment incentives

- Effects on other
  firms and markets

### Financial Issues

- Financing start-
  ups and acquisitions

- Effect on cost of
  capital

- Use of utility
  funds and credit

- Effect on utility
  financial condition

- Variability of
  earnings

- Investor
  reaction

SOURCE: National Association of Regulatory Utility Commissioners,
"1982 Report of the Ad Hoc Committee on Utility Diversification."

company's recent moves into the phone industry is that telecommunications "has changed from an increasing-cost to a decreasing-cost business, while electric power has been going the other way." 128/

According to economist Arthur Thompson, the economic case for electric utility diversification (of any kind) can be summed up in four arguments:

> (1) The returns which companies are able to earn in the electric utility industry do not justify the huge commitments of new capital which are being made--much greater profit potential for these dollar investments exists elsewhere; (2) there is growing risk that central-station generation of power may become economically or technologically obsolete (or both) well before the time present investments are depreciated and need to be replaced; (3) the market for conventionally generated electricity is on the verge of becoming a no-growth business, owing to the combined effects of higher rates, conservation, and searches for substitute forms of generation; and (4) it makes little strategic sense to confine a company's activities solely to a maturing industry which is a first-order cash-hog type business and that is characterized by increasing unit costs. 129/

Many analysts would add a fifth entry to Thompson's list--the fact that some diversification ventures could produce a synergistic improvement in either the utility's or the new venture's performance. Utility-owned coal mines, for instance, have an assured market for their production--an advantage that could result in greater efficiency than would be possible at an independent mine.

Another argument often advanced by those who look favorbly upon diversification is that by allowing utilities to get involved in unregulated businesses, where executive salaries are typically higher, diversification may offer utility managements more incentive to perform. "I think that one of the good things about utility diversification is that it might help attract good management," says Michael Foley, director of financial analysis for NARUC. 130/

Yet another argument favoring diversification is that investors tend to look on diversified utilities with more favor than undiversified utilities. Although this argument probably is not as strong today as it has been in recent years--because many utility diversification ventures have been in energy-related businesses that are now out of favor with investors--a number of recent studies indicate that utility diversification is still viewed positively in the stock market. A study released in 1982 by the Cabot Consulting Group, for instance, found that "diversification can make electric utility securities more attractive" and that diversified utilities tend to outperform their undiversified counterparts financially. 131/ Jennifer Proga, a utility analyst for Salomon Brothers, also surveyed utility performance and found that "market data indicate that investors are paying higher prices for the stocks of the most-diversified companies," thus giving these firms "some of the highest market-to-book ratios of the industry." 132/ Proga noted, however, that only the most highly diversified utilities--those that had diversified over a long period of time--tended to outperform the industry averages significantly. "When diversification of a utility accounts for 10 percent or less of its revenues, the company's market performance is not improved," she said. 133/

A final rationale cited for utility diversification efforts is an argument common to all undiversified businesses--that, aside from the question of the economic prospects for any particular business, diversification lessens risk by reducing dependence on any single line of business. While the empirical evidence to support this contention is somewhat shaky at best--indeed a number of studies of corporate conglomerates have found that diversification has actually increased levels of business risk--this argument remains a central part of the theory behind corporate strategic planning. In fact, the concept of diversification has become so entrenched in American business circles that a high level of diversification is now seen as the "normal" form for a mature corporation. 134/

## CHAPTER IV FOOTNOTES

1.  See, for instance, Carl F. Jaedicke, "Strategic Planning: A View from the Bottom Up," Public Utilities Fortnightly, Dec. 3, 1981, p. 52.

2.  "Credit Line Is Set for Philadelphia Electric Facility," The Wall Street Journal, July 22, 1983.

3.  Edison Electric Institute, press conference, Dec. 15, 1983.

4.  "A High-Risk Era for the Utilities," op. cit., p. 83.

5.  Mark Dodosh, "Cleveland Electric, Merrill Lynch Sell Bonds a New Way," The Wall Street Journal, May 27, 1980.

6.  "PG&E Pioneers New Cash Sources," Business Week, July 20, 1981, p. 149.

7.  Arthur Thompson, "The Strategic Dilemma of Electric Utilities--Part I," Public Utilities Fortnightly, March 18, 1982, p. 27.

8.  Bob Deans, "NYC Users Opt for Con Ed's Discount Rates," Energy User News, April 26, 1982, p. 4.

9.  "Utilities Are Tempting Big Customers To Turn Up The Juice," Business Week, Oct. 31, 1983, p. 121.

10. Robert Spann, electricity regulation seminar, Government Institutes Inc., Washington, D.C., March 2, 1983.

11. Paul Ingrassia, "American Electric Power, Long Protected, Finally Suffers from a Decline in Demand," The Wall Street Journal, Dec. 15, 1982, p. 33.

12. See Sally Hunt Streiter, "Trending the Rate Base," Public Utilities Fortnightly, May 13, 1982, p. 32.

13. Gerald S. Bower and Mark R. Berg, "The Changing Environment for Electric Power Generation: Portrait of a Transition," Public Utilities Fortnightly, July 22, 1982, pp. 27-28.

14. Douglas Cogan and Susan Williams, Generating Energy Alternatives: Conservation, Load Management and Renewable Energy at America's Electric Utilities (Investor Responsibility Research Center; Washington, D.C.; 1983.)

15. Thompson, op. cit., p. 28.

16. Keith L. Turley, "The Electric Utility Executives' Forum," Public Utilities Fortnightly, April 9, 1981, p. 78.

17. Robert Spann, electricity regulation seminar, Government Institutes Inc., Washington, D.C., March 3, 1983.

18. "Utilities Gear up for New Marketing Thrust," Electrical World, August 1982, p. 104.

19. William C. Hayes, "Marketing Could be the Key," Electrical World, November 1982, p. 3.

20. "Capping the Explosion in Gas Prices," Business Week, Dec. 20, 1982.

21. Ingrassia, op. cit., p. 33.

22. Arthur Thompson, ""The Strategic Dilemma of Electric Utilities--Part II," Public Utilities Fortnightly, April 1, 1982, p. 22.

23. Winston Williams, "Commonwealth Edison's Aim," The New York Times, Aug. 4, 1982, p. D1; also Commonwealth Edison Co., 1982 Form 10-K, Securities and Exchange Commission.

24. Bill Richards, "Chicago Utility Sharply Raises Cost of Delays," The Wall Street Journal, Jan. 26, 1984, p. 4; also Ron Winslow, "Records on Commonwealth Edison Show History of Nuclear Problems," The Wall Street Journal, Jan. 27, 1984, p. 33.

25. Sherwood H. Smith Jr., "The Electric Utility Executives' Forum," Public Utilities Fortnightly, April 9, 1981, p. 109.

26. Frances Cerra, "Lilco Uses Ads to Bring Case to Public," The New York Times, April 19, 1982, p. B2.

27. Advertising Age, May 9, 1983, p. 84.

28. "Three Utilities to Pay $130,500 to Michigan On Vote-Law Changes, The Wall Street Journal, March 10, 1983.

29. Arlen J. Large, "Nuclear Power Plant Advocates and Foes Start Battling Through TV Commercials," The Wall Street Journal, Dec. 9, 1982.

30. Fred Webber, EEI press conference, Dec. 15, 1983.

31. See for example Christopher Flavin, Nuclear Power: The Market Test (Worldwatch Institute; Washington, D.C.; 1983).

32. Bower and Berg, op. cit., p. 26; also findings from IRRC survey on alternative energy sources.

33. Response of Public Service Co. of New Mexico to IRRC survey, June 1982.

34. Robert Spann, interview with author, July 6, 1983.

35. Martha Hamilton, "Electricity Forecasts Debated," The Washington Post, June 4, 1983, p. C1.

36. A. David Rossin, personal correspondence to author, July 1, 1980.

37. Marshall McDonald, "The Hemorrhage of Inflation," Public Utilities Fortnightly, April 9, 1981, p. 19.

38. Robert M. Bigwood, "The Electric Utility Executives' Forum," Public Utilities Fortnightly, April 9, 1981, p. 69.

39. "Washington and the Utilities," Public Utilities Fortnightly, Aug. 5, 1982, p. 46.

40. Peter Navarro, "Our Stake in the Electric Utility's Dilemma," Harvard Business Review, May-June 1982, p. 87.

41. Ibid.

42. See U.S. Department of Energy, The Future of Electric Power in America: Economic Supply for Economic Growth, Office of Policy, Planning and Analysis, June 1983.

43. Don D. Jordan, "A Struggle We Have to Win," Public Utilities Fortnightly, June 9, 1983, p. 22.

44. Navarro, op. cit., p. 93.

45. Ibid., p. 94.

46. "Recession Causes Industry's First Decline in Peak," Electrical World, September 1982, p. 84.

47. Don C. Frisbee and M. Eugene Akridge, "The State of the Utility Management Art: Emerging Utility Strategies," Public Utilities Fortnightly, March 12, 1981, p. 15.

48. Energy Information Administration, "Statistics of Privately Owned Electric Utilities, 1981 Annual," June 1983, p. 513; also Consolidated Edison, 1982 annual report.

49. Cancellations figures were compiled from various sources including the Atomic Industrial Forum, the Edison Electric Institute and the Energy Information Administration.

50. "Peak growth returns as both economy and temperatures heat up," Electrical World, September 1983, p. 61.

51. "The Vicious Circle That Utilities Can't Seem To Break," Business Week, May 23, 1983, p. 178.

52. John V. Thornton, "Increased Public Ownership of Electric Utilities: A Step in the Wrong Direction," Public Utilities Fortnightly, July 16, 1981, p. 16; various other sources.

53. Ibid., p. 17.

54. Gordon D. Friedlander, "New Life Available for Old T/Gs and Boilers," Electrical World, May 1983, p. 87.

55. Anthony F. Bavington, "Uprating Old Units Pays Off," Public Power, March-April 1983, p. 68.

56. Alex Radin, "Strategies for the Future," Public Power, November-December 1982, p. 8.

57. Friedlander, op. cit., p. 87.

58. Alan Miller, personal correspondence to author, Dec. 7, 1983.

59. Pamela J. Ruben, "Utility Plans to Mandate Conservation for New Users," Energy User News, Nov. 16, 1981, p. 1.

60. Duke Power Co., 1982 Proxy Statement, p. 16.

61. Amory and Hunter Lovins, "Electric Utilities: Key to Capitalizing the Energy Transition," draft of Mitchell Prize competition entry, 1982, p. 14.

62. Robert F. Hemphill Jr., "Testimony before the U.S. House Committee on Public Works and Transportation," Sept. 12, 1979.

63. Douglas Cogan and Susan Williams, op. cit., p. 7.

64. "Joint Action Ventures Seen as a Way to Stop Spiraling Electric Power Costs," Public Utilities Fortnightly, May 7, 1981, p. 49.

65. Forbes, May 28, 1979, p. 92.

66. Tom Watson, presentation at electricity regulation seminar, Government Institutes Inc., March 3, 1983.

67. Douglas Cogan and Susan Williams, op. cit., p. 8.

68. S.J. Nola, chief generation planning engineer for Southern California Edison, letter to IRRC, Aug. 12, 1982.

69. Jeff Barber, "Govt. to Buy Low-Cost Energy From Non-Utility Sources," Energy User News, April 4, 1983, p. 13.

70. General Public Utilities Corp., 1981 Annual Report, p. 3.

71. Alyssa A. Lappen, "Electric Utilities," Forbes, Jan. 5, 1981, p. 217.

72. W. Reid Thompson, "The Electric Utility Executives' Forum," Public Utilities Fortnightly, April 9, 1981, p. 77.

73. Peter Hunt, conversation with author, Nov. 18, 1983.

74. Geraldine Brooks et al., "Utilities Face a Crisis Over Nuclear Plants; Cost, Delays Mount," The Wall Street Journal, Dec. 1, 1983, p. 1.

75. Peter Navarro, "The Soft, Hard, or Smart Path: Charting the Electric Utility Industry's Future," Public Utilities Fortnightly, June 18, 1981, p. 25.

76. Douglas N. Jones, "Letter to the Editor," Harvard Business Review, September-October 1982, p. 180.

77. Andrew Reynolds, "Letter to the Editor," Harvard Business Review, September-October 1982, p. 174.

78. Irwin Stelzer and David B. Roe, "Viewpoint," Electrical World, May 1982, p. 59.

79. Charles M. Studness, "Utility Stock Offerings and Book Values," Public Utilities Fortnightly, Feb. 26, 1981, p. 50.

80. William R. Gould, memorandum to all employees, Oct. 9, 1980.

81. Southern California Edison, 1981 and 1982 annual reports.

82. "PG&E Shifts to Renewables in 1980s," Energy Users Report, April 29, 1982, p. 431; also Pacific Gas & Electric, 1981 and 1982 annual reports and "Long-Term Planning Results 1983-2002."

83. Responses of Pacific Gas & Electric and Southern California Edison to IRRC survey, 1982.

84. Laurel Leff, "S. California Edison Raises Commitment to Alternative Energy in 'Major Change'," The Wall Street Journal, Oct. 20, 1980, p. 21.

85. Gerald F. Tape, "Electric Utility R&D Requirements in the 1980s," Public Utilities Fortnightly, April 9, 1981, p. 36.

86. Ibid., p. 37.

87. Alfred H. Canada, "Solar Voltaic Generator Requirements for Large-Scale Central Generation," Paper No. P3-14B-1, 16th Photovoltaic Specialists Conference, San Diego, Sept. 29, 1982.

88. Mark Weaver, "Low Calif. Buy-Back Rates May Harm Cogen.," Energy User News, Nov. 14, 1983, p. 14.

89. Leff, op. cit.

90. Ibid.

91. Jane Bergler, speech before the American Society of Civil Engineers, May 18, 1983.

92. Quoted in "A Major Change in the Way We Do Business," Not Man Apart, November 1980, p. 17.

93. Stelzer and Roe, op. cit., p. 59.

94. "The Vicious Circle. . . .," op. cit., p. 188.

95. Radin, op. cit., p. 6.

96. Leff, op. cit.

97. Ray Vicker, "PG&E Hopes to be Buying Electricity from Biggest U.S. 'Wind Farm' by 1985," The Wall Street Journal, Nov. 11, 1982, p. 20.

98. Thompson, op. cit., p. 23.

99. Radin, op. cit., p. 8

100. Jerry L. Maulden, "The Electric Utility Executives' Forum," Public Utilities Fortnightly, April 9, 1981, p. 92.

101. H.A. Cavanaugh, "Utilities Search for New Revenue Sources," Electrical World, July 1981, p. 40.

102. "A High-Risk Era for the Utilities," Business Week, Feb. 23, 1981, p. 76.

103. Cavanaugh, op. cit., p. 39.

104. John R. Emshwiller, "Electric Utilities' Moves Into Other Businesses Are Viewed With Skepticism on Wall Street," The Wall Street Journal, Aug. 11, 1982, p. 45.

105. Ibid.

106. J. Robert Malko, interview with author, May 23, 1983.

107. Keystone Coal Industry Manual and U.S. Department of Energy, Energy Information Administration, "Directory of Coal Production Ownership, 1979," October 1981, pp. 2-3.

108. New England Electric System, 1982 Form 10-K, pp. 16-17; also "NEESPLAN 1980-1995," Introduction and Executive Summary, October 1979, pp. 5-6.

109. See "OGJ Report," Oil & Gas Journal, Oct. 17, 1983, p. 80.

110. "Winds of Change at Wisconsin Power & Light," Power Line, November 1982, p. 4.

111. "Consumers Will Benefit If Utilities Are Allowed To Diversify, Consultant Says," Energy Users Report, Oct. 20, 1983, p. 1006.

112. Robert A. Lincicome, "1984 To Be Year of Financial Rebuilding, Reduced Construction Spending for Utilities," Electric Light & Power, December 1983, p. 16.

113. Pamela J. Ruben, "Utilities Enter Energy Gear Sales Market," Energy User News, Aug. 31, 1981, p. 1.

114. "Official Says Marketing Conservation Good Source of Earnings For Utilities," Energy Users Report, May 26, 1983, p. 522.

115. Public Service Electric & Gas Co., 1982 annual report, p. 22.

116. Ron Scherer, "U.S. Utilities, with Plenty of Warm Water, Begin Raising Fish," The Christian Science Monitor, June 19, 1980, p. 11.

117. Lovins, op. cit., p. 10.

118. "EEI Plans Seminars on Potential of Various Fields for Utility Diversification," Public Utilities Fortnightly, Jan. 6, 1983, p. 20.

119. H.A. Cavanaugh, op. cit., p. 41.

120. H.A. Cavanaugh, "Diversification: How Free Will Your Moves Be?" Electrical World, November 1981, p. 40.

121. See "Utilities Buck the Trend to Diversify," Business Week, Dec. 14, 1981, p. 132.

122. "A High-Risk Era for the Utilities," op. cit., p. 78.

123. Richard Mullen, "Utils. Eye FERC-Ruled Subsidiaries To Hike Rates," Energy User News, Sept. 26, 1983, p. 1.

124. J. Robert Malko, interview with author, May 23, 1983.

125. Ibid.

126. Donald C. Bauer, "Alternate Responses to the Financial Crisis in the Electric Utility Industry," October 1981, p. 22.

127. J. Robert Malko, presentation before the Ninth Annual National Utilities Conference, Chicago, May 13, 1981.

128. "A High-Risk Era for the Utilities," op. cit., p. 77.

129. Thompson, op. cit., Part II, p. 22.

130. Michael Foley, interview with author, August 10, 1983.

131. "New Study Supports Diversification," Electrical World, June 1982, p. 52.

132. See "Can Diversification Really Work," Electrical World, January 1982, p. 55.

133. Ibid.

134. See for instance, Kenneth R. Andrews, The Concept of Corporate Strategy (Richard D. Irwin, Inc.; Homewood, Ill.; 1980), p. 60.

# V
# OPTIONS FOR STRUCTURAL CHANGES IN
# ELECTRIC POWER REGULATION

### Debate over Regulation

Few issues in the debate over the electric utility industry's future are as critical or as politically charged as those surrounding utility regulation. Regulation in general--as well as the specifics of how it is applied in the electric power industry--is currently under attack from many sides. A number of major industries, including the railroads, airlines, interstate trucking, natural gas and telecommunications, have recently undergone partial or total deregulation.

The impetus for regulatory reform comes from many directions and from conflicting objectives. Many consumers believe that the rapid rise in electric rates over the last decade indicates that their state utility commissions have been co-opted by the utilities they are supposed to regulate. Conversely, the industry and the investment community tend to perceive regulators as being too politically motivated to allow utilities to earn a fair rate of return and as a source of interminable delay. Overarching this debate are questions about whether the original economic conditions that led to regulation in the utility industry remain operative and to what extent electricity is a basic entitlement of consumers as opposed to a product that they may choose to buy. This chapter briefly describes some perceptions about the state of the existing regulatory system and explores several of the most prominent alternatives for the structural reform of electric utility regulation. While it is not realistic to expect any of the alternatives to be adopted in full, the gradual introduction of elements of various proposals appears likely.

The purpose of regulation: The concept behind the existing electric utility regulatory system is relatively simple: electric power generation and distribution is a natural monopoly because it is characterized by decreasing long run costs, is exceedingly capital intensive and has enormous economies of scale. Thus, to allow various firms to compete and duplicate each other's facilities in a given service area would be inordinately inefficient and could impair the industry's ability to serve its customers. Competition between firms, which ordinarily is expected to breed efficiency and protect consumers from monopolistic pricing, must therefore be simulated for a single firm by regulation. As economist Alfred Kahn puts it, "The essence of regulation is the explicit replacement of competition with governmental orders as the principal institutional device for assuring good service." 1/

Utility commissions have typically been seen as having only a very limited role in power planning decisions. In theory, the duty of a public utility commission has generally been to set rates at a level so that the utility's overall level of revenues covers operating costs and earns a "just and reasonable" return for investors. In determining the appropriate level of return, regulators are expected to assess the returns available on competing investments with similar degrees of business and financial risk. In practice, however, the concept of "cost of service" ratemaking has historically been applied somewhat arbitrarily. For many years during the post World War II era, regulators tended to set levels of return that were well in excess of the industry's cost of capital. In recent years, many utilities have earned returns that are below their cost of capital. In addition, many commissions have come to believe that they have an important oversight role to ensure proper management decisions.

The question of what constitutes good regulation is an important one and tends to color perceptions of the current debate over utility regulation. Many industry executives note that although the tools of economic analysis have improved immensely since the first state regulatory commissions were set up in 1907, regulators in some states still rely more on their political instincts and on seat of the pants judgments than on serious economic analysis in setting rates. Moreover, managers tend to view the entrance of regulators into the utility planning process as a dangerous and unnecessary intrusion into management's affairs. But consumers are quick to point out that poor management decisions by segments of the industry are evident and that utilities have coerced the public into wasting billions of dollars on canceled or unneeded generating plants. Meanwhile, investors typically rate regulatory agencies predominantly on the basis of how large a rate of return they authorize. According to the latest semiannual ranking of state regulatory environments by Salomon Brothers, no regulatory commissions deserve an "A" ranking.

In spite of all this disagreement, there is growing recognition that regardless of what good regulation is supposed to be in theory, utility managers and regulators both have a stake in cooperating to make certain that correct decisions get made and implemented. Leonard Hyman, a utility analyst with Merrill Lynch, has made this point.

> Is good regulation a ratification of management's deci-
> sions? On a short run basis, that might be the way investors
> should look at the matter. . . . On the other hand, a regu-
> latory agency that simply sits back while utilities make all
> sorts of decisions that could have unfortunate results in the
> future isn't doing consumers or security holders any favors.
> We should not assume that utility managements have the
> exclusive insight into what is correct. 2/

Perceptions of the problem: There is currently a relatively widespread perception that electric utility regulation is not working very
well. Beyond this agreement, however, there is little consensus as to
why the present system is not working and what, if anything, should
be done about it. The complaints about regulation come from all
sides of the political and economic spectrum and are too numerous to
discuss in detail. Among the most fundamental arguments, however,
are the following:

-- The "natural monopoly" rationale for regulation in the electric
   power industry is now inoperative because economies of scale
   no longer exist and competition from small-scale decentralized power sources is increasingly evident. The existing regulatory system is outmoded because it was designed to work in
   a low-inflation environment. Therefore, the regulatory process should be scrapped entirely or modified to take into
   account the new economic conditions in the industry. This
   may entail transitional problems but ultimately will lead to
   increased overall efficiency and better financial performance
   for well-managed utilities. A number of economists and
   industry consulting groups and a few utilities hold this perspective.

-- Politicized regulation is seriously harming the financial health
   of the industry. This is leading to underinvestment in new
   capacity, the promotion of inefficient energy strategies and
   probable electricity supply shortages in the 1990s. Thus,
   sweeping structural reform of the current regulatory system,
   perhaps involving expanded federal powers, is necessary to
   limit political pressures on regulators, promote investment in
   new plants and protect consumers from shortages. This argument is advanced in recent work by the Department of Energy
   and is supported by some segments of the electric power
   industry.

-- Electric utilities have become multi-state conglomerates that
   have outgrown the legal and accounting abilities of the state-
   based regulatory system. Regulatory commissions need to be
   sheltered from political squabbles and funded adequately.
   Modest regulatory reforms are needed to improve the coordi-

nation between state regulatory bodies, reduce discrepancies and conflicts between states, provide incentives for management efficiency and promote equitable treatment of companies and consumers. Many state legislators and regulators and a few utility managers support this view.

-- Electricity is a vital service that has become a basic right of citizens. Principles of fairness must temper the debate over maximum efficiency in this industry. Current regulation is not doing enough to protect consumers from excessive rate increases and bad management decisions. Thus, regulation must be made more responsive to social welfare concerns through the legislative process, referenda and other public forums. In the absence of meaningful reforms, perhaps industry planning and even ownership should be taken over by the government. This position is taken by a number of consumer and public interest groups and is becoming increasingly popular among state politicians.

## Options For Structural Reform

While many of the complaints about the existing utility regulatory system have been around for some time, it is only in the last several years that a number of relatively specific proposals for tackling these problems have surfaced. This section discusses four of the most common ideas for structural reform--deregulation, federal preemption of utility regulation, regionalization of power planning and regulation, and government ownership. Some of these proposals remain theoretical, with little broad support or political feasibility. Elements of other proposals, however, have attracted considerable attention and are already beginning to be implemented in limited regulatory experiments. All of the proposals have a number of variants and none is considered acceptable by all of the affected parties.

Deregulation: A variety of proposals call for deregulation of the electric power industry in varying degrees. Most of these proposals have a number of common elements, however. The premise of all deregulatory proposals is that they will result in competition that will, in the long run at least, promote efficiency and protect consumers.

One important assumption of most deregulation proposals is that the three major functions performed by today's vertically integrated utilities--generation, transmission and distribution--are distinct from an economic standpoint and should be separated. Likewise, virtually all deregulation proposals assume that the distribution of electricity continues to be a natural monopoly and therefore should continue to be regulated. In addition, they usually assume an independent transmission stage that, whether subject to regulation or government-owned, would purchase power from competing generating companies and sell it to distribution companies on a fair and nondiscriminatory basis. The major areas of difference between the various deregulation options that have been proposed, therefore, are in the degree and timing of deregulation of the generating portion of the industry. Four of these proposals are outlined below. 3/ Deregulation of the entire electric power business is an idea that is so fraught with legal problems and has such limited support that it will not even be discussed.

Total deregulation of power generation--The most radical proposal calls for total deregulation of all generating units through asset sell-offs or generating company spin-offs. Once completed, companies would be free to sell power from old and new generating units at whatever price the market would bear, probably resulting in significant price increases in the short term. The transitional problems from this approach could be considerable, proponents acknowledge, but they support it because they believe high cost generating plants would quickly be out of business; producers would have an incentive to build and operate low-cost, efficient plants; construction of unneeded plants would be discouraged; and in the longer term, efficiency gains would result in lower prices. 4/

Deregulation of new plants--This is a partial deregulation approach in which existing generating units would remain subject to regulation but new generating units of any size would be allowed to receive market (or avoided cost) prices for their output. Utilities would be allowed to set up unregulated subsidiaries to invest in new plants but they would have to compete with anyone else that was willing to enter this market. The transitional problems would be somewhat less from this approach than from total deregulation, yet market forces would still determine when and which new plants get built. 5/

Transactions deregulation--This type of deregulation involves deregulating only certain bulk transactions, such as wholesale power sales between utility companies or service to certain classes of customers. In effect, FERC regulation of wholesale power transactions would be eliminated and distribution companies would be free to shop for the lowest price electricity for resale to their customers. All transactions, however, would remain subject to approval by state commissions. Short term "spot market" power brokerages could be established and could eventually be extended to longer-term transactions. Transactions deregulation has already been approved in two limited FERC experiments involving six Southwestern utilities and several utilities in Florida. 6/ Adoption of this option would result in only minimal transitional problems, but it would not address many of the perceived problems with the existing regulatory system.

Incremental asset deregulation--This approach involves a series of gradual steps to free up the value and increase the mobility of generating plant assets. Utilities could be given freedom to participate fully in small power production; rules governing utility mergers and takeovers and diversification could be loosened; and utilities could be allowed to buy or sell assets at their market values, without regard to their original cost. This proposal could be coupled with transactions deregulation. By phasing in the deregulation process over a period of time, this approach might ease some transitional problems but yield fewer of deregulation's postulated benefits. 7/

Problems and prospects--The concept of deregulation has received widespread attention in the electric power industry in recent years as a result of the trend toward deregulation in other industries and the growing financial difficulties of some segments of the industry. In practical terms, however, deregulation of electric utilities faces some formidable obstacles.

First, there is no widespread consensus within the industry itself that deregulation would be desirable or would solve the financial problems that are at the center of the debate over regulatory reforms. Only one utility chief executive officer has endorsed the most sweeping deregulation option outlined above. Many private utilities are loath to participate in an experiment that could lead to a number of bankruptcies in the industry and might spark additional demands for public power. Nor have public power agencies shown much enthusiasm for deregulating electric generation.

Second, the legal and economic problems posed by vertical disintegration of utility companies would be extremely difficult, if not insurmountable. A number of observers have noted that the unique features of the utility industry's capitalization, with an astronomical amount of mortgage bonds and preferred stocks outstanding, make the voluntary vertical disintegration of the industry virtually impossible. 8/ Comprehensive federal legislation mandating the breakup of the industry would be needed and would probably face enormous opposition.

Third, the more comprehensive deregulation proposals raise concerns about reliability, loss of coordination among systems, reduced overall efficiency and difficulties in financing. 9/ All of these might result in higher costs to the consumer and the need to reregulate the industry.

Finally, the political problems facing deregulation of electric utilities are compounded by the industry's history of state regulation. The electric power industry cannot be deregulated through the abolition of a federal agency or the modification of rules governing interstate commerce--as happened in the airline, trucking and railroad industries--because of the pervasive, and in many cases zealously guarded, powers of the state regulatory system.

Comprehensive deregulation of the electric power industry is clearly a much more difficult process than the deregulation that is taking place in other industries. "In the airline industry, potential entrants were queued up, assets were easily transferable from market to market, and entry lead times were short," notes Irwin Stelzer, president of National Economic Research Associates. "Not so in the electric power business, where existing firms are trying to diversify out of the business, where assets don't have wings, and where entry times are as long as 12 years." 10/ As the issue of comprehensive electric power deregulation has received increased study, many observers have concluded that more problems have been uncovered than solutions and that some of the initial momentum behind the idea is fading. "The talk about [electric utility] deregulation was more in vogue in 1981 than it is now," says Stanley York, a commissioner with the Wisconsin Public Service Commission. 11/

But while the political, economic and legal obstacles to comprehensive deregulation are nothing short of monumental, efforts to introduce competition into electricity markets in a limited way are likely to continue if only because the status quo is almost uniformly unpopular, consumers will continue to pressure Congress and the competitive elements already fostered by PURPA may snowball beyond expectations. "What members learn in their fast education on gas markets in 1983 will inevitably spill over into electricity issues," says Chris Warner, minority counsel to the House Subcommittee on Energy Conservation and Power. "If Congress perceives there is an oversupply but prices are still going up," Warner says, "you're going to see more interest in ways to generate competition." 12/ "There's an analogy here to the telecommunications industry," adds utility consultant Robert Spann. "All of these small power producers and cogenerators are just like MCI," concludes Spann, "so I advise utilities to consider deregulation a 20 to 25 percent chance for planning purposes." 13/

Federal preemption: A second proposed approach to the problems with the existing utility regulatory system involves a larger federal role in electricity supply planning and retail rate regulation. A number of analysts who subscribe to the notion that "underinvestment" by electric utilities is a serious problem that may lead to shortages have proposed variants of this solution. Implicit in this approach is the assumption that regulation at the state level is not working for various political reasons and that federal regulators would be able to do a better job. Basically, federal preemption could be implemented in two ways: 1) directly, through the complete preemption of state regulation by FERC; or 2) indirectly, through the establishment of uniform federal standards that state commissions would have to follow in setting rates.

Direct preemption--Complete federal preemption of retail rate regulation, proponents argue, would reduce many of the political problems engendered by regulation at the state level and would ensure uniformity and consistency in regulation. The process might also reduce administrative inefficiency by eliminating the duplication inherent in 50 state regulatory commissions and staffs. Federal regulators might also be better equipped to handle such questions as the need for new generating units, it is argued, because they would be able to coordinate power supply planning between neighboring states. While it is generally acknowledged that this form of federal preemption would face massive opposition from the states and probably from much of the industry, even the existence of this proposal is seen by some observers as having a sobering effect on state regulators. "The mere threat of nationalizing utility regulation under the FERC might be enough to prompt state PUCs to act on their own," writes pre-emption advocate Peter Navarro. 14/

Indirect preemption--This approach would use mandatory federal standards imposed on state regulators to ensure fairness and unifor-mity. The mandatory standards relate to procedural issues such the inclusion of construction work in progress (CWIP) in the rate base, normalization of tax benefits, limitations on regulatory lag, and the use of future test years. Proponents of this approach also see it as a means to reduce the politicization of the ratemaking process and promote uniformity in state regulation, but without the need for a new or greatly expanded federal bureaucracy.

Problems and prospects--The major problem with proposals that give the federal government a greater role in electric utility regu-lation is political. Such proposals run against the states' rights ori-entation of the Reagan administration and the current mood in Con-gress. The direct preemption option--with its inherent logic that the federal government can regulate better than the states--is seen as politically impossible for the Reagan administration. Moreover, most political observers believe that even a change in administrations would not be enough to overcome the opposition to this approach. "Congress has not had to touch the retail electric rate controversy for a long time and it doesn't want to start now," notes Chris Warner. "You won't see any electricity legislation addressing this problem," Warner predicts. 15/

Even the indirect preemption option is seen as facing enormous political difficulties. According to a recent report by the National Governors' Association, indirect preemption "would enjoy a limited political constituency on Capitol Hill and in the industry but would be inconsistent with the [Reagan] administration's new federalism em-phasis." 16/ The NGA report sums up the prospects for preemptive approaches to utility regulatory reform as poor, stating: "Judging from the Carter administration's failure to win congressional ap-proval of a preemptive utility reform package in 1977-78 and the current administration's overt concern to avoid preemptive ap-proaches to electric utility issues, it seems clear that a non-preemp-tive criterion enjoys wide support in the Congress and the admins-tration." 17/

The political roadblocks to preemptive strategies for reforming electric power regulation do not preclude a continued aggressive ef-fort on the part of Congress and the administration to aid utilities through tax benefits, federal procedural rulings and attempts to persuade states to implement regulatory changes. The Economic Recovery Tax Act of 1981, for instance, included a number of sig-nificant tax benefits for utilities and utility investors. Similarly, the Federal Energy Regulatory Commission voted in 1983 to allow utilities to charge wholesale customers for plants under construction by including up to 50 percent of their construction work in progress costs in the rate base. Such a ruling by FERC could have a significant influence on state regulations because a number of states use FERC as a model for their own rulings on procedural issues.

Finally, two moderately preemptive strategies exist that would increase the federal role in utility regulation yet might garner support from the Reagan administration precisely because they could be cloaked as moves toward deregulation. First, if Congress were to approve a major loosening of the Public Utility Holding Company Act (PUHCA), which is supported by the SEC, the effect could be to allow utilities to choose whether they were regulated by FERC or by the states. Utilities, if given permission to form holding companies by state regulators, could sell power from generating companies to operating subsidiaries and effectively opt out of regulation in any state where regulators were unfriendly. Alternatively, legislation facilitating the creation of regional electric generation companies could have the same effect. Utilities could pool resources to build new generating units under the auspices of regional generating companies whose power sales would be subject to FERC regulation. 18/ Either of these developments could potentially allow utilities to shift the primary review of future ratemaking from the states to FERC.

Implementation of either of these alternatives would probably require the assent of state regulators. A surprising degree of support from state regulators for the concept of generating companies might well be forthcoming, however, even though it would raise rates in the short run. Many regulators believe that the concept would eventually result in increased competition from other private generators, holding rates down in the long run.

Regional power planning and regulation: A third major option for structural regulatory reform involves regional power planning and perhaps regional regulation. In its most severe form, this would involve legislation preempting both state and FERC rate regulation in favor of a new system of regional regulatory commissions. Since this scenario is considered extremely unlikely from a political standpoint, however, this section will concentrate on proposals for voluntary regionalization of the power planning and regulatory processes.

The concept of a voluntary program to enable states to move gradually toward multistate power planning, and eventually regulation, has been gaining support recently as a non-preemptive alternative to deregulation or federal preemption. This idea was endorsed in 1983 by the National Governors' Association task force on utility regulation as a concept that would solve many of the existing regulatory system's perceived problems and might be acceptable to many states. 20/ "State regulators need to have the ability to look at the whole picture, to make judgments based on regional regulatory approaches," says Edward Helme, staff director of the NGA study group. 21/

## UPDATE ON PUHCA REFORM

The Public Utilities Holding Company Act of 1935 is a relatively little known law that makes certain business practices of utility holding companies subject to regulation by the Securities and Exchange Commission. PUHCA was a product of Franklin Roosevelt's New Deal campaign against the abuses of early utility holding companies, practices such as the sale of services and properties within the system at inflated prices and pyramid corporate structures that allowed a few individuals to dominate the industry.

For the last three years, investor-owned utilities have conducted a major lobbying campaign to repeal or modify PUHCA on the grounds that its restrictions are no longer needed from a consumer protection standpoint and unnecessarily burden the utilities. Outright repeal of PUHCA is backed by the SEC and the Department of Energy. The movement to repeal PUHCA ran into such vigorous opposition in 1983 from consumers, small business contractors and the National Association of Regulatory Utility Commissioners (NARUC), however, that repeal is no longer considered politically feasible.

Nevertheless, the industry continues to consider modifications to PUHCA a top priority and has worked out a compromise plan that is acceptable to small business interests and will not be opposed by NARUC. "The issue is not diversification," says William Grigg, executive vice president of Duke Power, "diversification is already taking place. But we believe the holding company structure is the most desirable way to do this." 19/ Among the most significant provisions of the compromise are ones that would: permit holding companies to invest in unrelated businesses unless a state files a complaint, permit loans and market rate service contracts between operating subsidiaries and holding companies, remove SEC oversight of securities issuances unless a state complains, and grandfather existing SEC exemptions.

The outlook for passage of a PUHCA compromise is clouded. Some gas utilities and publicly owned utilities and some key congressmen remain opposed to the bill.

As noted in Chapter II, multistate power pools and other forms of informal regional power planning are already well established in many areas of the country. This process could be further fostered, say proponents of regionalization, by the passage of federal legislation allowing states to form regional organizations responsible for such activities as supply and demand forecasting, regional reliability and reserve requirements, energy conservation plans, and coordination with other systems. Decisions on exactly which activities states would cede to these regional organizations would be left to the states, with those participating ratifying a compact. State legislators would also retain discretion to decide whether regional supply plans would be binding on utilities and state PUCs.

Regional planning could result in immediate efficiency improvements and could be financed through a uniform assessment on utilities in participating states, its proponents say. Moreover, as states gradually became comfortable with regional power planning, it could be coupled with regional regulation. States could begin to delegate accounting and procedural issues, such as the treatment of construction work in progress and fuel adjustment clauses, to the regional organization. Later, at their option, states could delegate more substantive powers and the regional commissions could take over FERC's role in regulating wholesale transactions--perhaps leading eventually to full-fledged regional regulation.

Problems and prospects--Regionalization of utility planning appears to offer a number of advantages from an economic efficiency perspective and is likely to continue to gain adherents in many regions. The political advantages of a gradual move toward regional planning and regulation also appear to be considerable in comparison with comprehensive deregulation or federal preemption. Nevertheless, this approach also has a number of drawbacks. First, a gradual change in utility regulation would clearly be of little help to those utilities that are already in desperate financial shape. Second, it is far from clear that the idea of regional regulation is something that most states would welcome. States tend to guard their powers zealously against real or perceived incursions from higher levels of government. "The good thing about regional regulation is that it would depoliticize the regulatory process," says Robert Malko of the Wisconsin Public Service Commission. "The problem is that the size of these regulatory bodies could lead to stagnation. In any case, state legislatures won't go for it." 22/

The regionalization approach may face additional obstacles at this time as a result of the current upheaval in the industry. The ramifications of several recent failures involving regional power planning and supply--such as the controversy involving the Washington Public Power Supply System and the Bonneville Power Administration in the Pacific Northwest--are still working their way into the public consciousness. Meanwhile, consumer groups, which are lobbying hard for elected utility commissions and utility regulation that is more responsive to consumer concerns, are likely to oppose vehemently the creation of new regulatory bodies that they would view as less accountable to the public. Finally, utilities themselves might be unsupportive of regional regulation if they felt that it would lead to greater uncertainties or that an entire region could become dominated by unfriendly regulators.

Public takeovers or financing: A final option for structural reform of regulation involves greater federal or state participation in the industry through takeovers of privately owned systems and/or publicly financed investments in new generating and transmission facilities. By putting increased responsibility for power planning, plant financing and rate regulation directly in the hands of state or federal agencies, this option would obviate worries that the investment returns available in the industry were too low to induce private companies to build sufficient generating capacity. This approach continues to receive considerable attention from consumers, state governments and other parties, although its supporters tend to like it for different reasons.

As noted in Chapters II and IV, public power is already expanding rapidly as more municipalities opt for it and as municipal and cooperative utilities buy into generating units under construction and build small new units. This trend could accelerate if federal and state public power agencies begin to expand the reach of their systems or take on a regional planning role. A significant expansion of federal public power is already under way in the Pacific Northwest as a result of the Northwest Power Act of 1981. The law, passed near the end of the Carter administration, established a regional planning council appointed by the governors of Oregon, Washington, Montana and Idaho and effectively makes the Bonneville Power Administration the planner and financier of new power plants in the region.

Similarly, government organizations seem headed toward a greater role in power planning and generation in New York State and New England. In New York State, the Power Authority of the State of New York (PASNY) currently generates nearly 30 percent of the electric power generated in the state. PASNY was originally set up to tap the abundant hydroelectric resources of the St. Lawrence River, but it now owns two nuclear units and several oil-fired units as well. In 1975, the Authority bought the Indian Point 3 nuclear unit from Consolidated Edison to help the company out of a financial bind. Now, New York Gov. Mario Cuomo is examining the option of having PASNY buy all or part of Long Island Lighting's $4 billion Shoreham unit to help shield customers on Long Island from massive rate increases and keep Lilco solvent. In addition, PASNY is positioning itself as the primary conduit for the the importation of Canadian hydroelectric power into New York State. Two other state agencies--the state energy office and the New York State Energy Research and Development Authority--are also playing an increasingly important role in planning energy development efforts and in coordinating energy R&D efforts.

In New England, consideration is being given to having a group of states use tax-exempt financing to finance jointly new generation or transmission facilities. This could involve the financing of investor-owned utility projects, direct financing of Canadian hydropower development for export to the region, or a regional organization to purchase Canadian power for resale to utilities.

Problems and prospects--The major problem with this option is its political infeasibility. Although state or regional public power agencies are likely to continue to consolidate their control over the electric power industry in some areas, these situations tend to occur where public power entities were established during the 1930s and are unlikely to be duplicated elsewhere. An increased public power role in regional planning and regulation is viewed as a step toward the nationalization of the industry in many circles, and would face enormous opposition from Congress, the investor-owned segment of the industry and the Reagan administration. Thus, while public power in various forms is likely to continue to chip away at the privately owned utilities' share of the market, it is unlikely to become a nationwide model for the reform of electric utility regulation.

Conclusions: The dissatisfaction with the existing electric utility regulatory system is real and will inevitably lead to modifications in this system. No comprehensive idea for structural reform of the system has yet emerged, however, that is both economically and politically feasible. The current regulatory system is clearly highly politicized, leading to hardship for many companies. But regulation is also propping up some companies that would probably be unable to survive in a more competitive environment. Thus, it will be hard to form a consensus behind most proposals for reform, even within the utility industry itself.

Elements from a variety of regulatory reform proposals are currently being implemented on a case-by-case or experimental basis. Such experiments are likely to continue and will no doubt lead to some permanent changes, but most of these reforms will be evolutionary. Among the most important of these changes are a movement toward wholesale power deregulation, greater use of multistate power planning, some loosening of restrictions on utility diversification, and the continued growth of public power. None of these changes will do much to aid those utilities that are truly in weak financial shape. In fact, the effect of a number of these changes will be to accelerate the rate at which competitive elements are introduced into electricity markets. From a financial performance standpoint, some of the most meaningful near term regulatory reforms are likely to emerge as a result of increased cooperation between utilities and regulatory staffs in the areas of power planning and utility business strategies. Such cooperation will be possible, however, only in states that have well-funded, professional public utility commission staffs that are relatively insulated from political pressures.

## CHAPTER V FOOTNOTES

1.  Alfred E. Kahn, The Economics of Regulation: Principles and Institutions (New York; John Wiley & Sons; 1970), Vol. 1, p. 20.

2.  Leonard S. Hyman, "Utility Research: Recent Regulatory Decisions and Trends," Merrill Lynch Pierce Fenner and Smith, Inc., May 1980, p. 2.

3.  For a more detailed discussion of all these options see James L. Plummer, editor, Electric Power Strategic Issues: Deregulation and Diversification (Public Utilities Reports and QED Research, 1983); also National Governors' Association, "An Analysis of Options For Structural Reform In Electric Utility Regulation," January 1983.

4.  See for instance, William W. Berry, "The Case for Competition in the Electric Utility Industry," Public Utilities Fortnightly, Sept. 16, 1982, p. 13.

5.  See for instance, Michael B. Meyer, "A Modest Proposal for the Partial Deregulation of Electric Utilities," Public Utilities Fortnightly, April 14, 1983, pp. 23-26.

6.  See for instance, "Bulk Power Market Experiments At The Federal Energy Regulatory Commission," FERC, Nov. 4, 1982; also Andy Pasztor, "Electricity Decontrol Test Cleared by U.S.; 6 Utilities to Set Own Rates in 2-Year Trial," The Wall Street Journal, Jan. 4, 1984, p. 6.

7.  See James L. Plummer, "A Different Approach to Electricity Deregulation," Public Utilities Fortnightly, July 7, 1983, pp. 16-20; also William W. Scranton III, "Reforming and Improving Utility Regulation," Public Utilities Fortnightly, Aug. 4, 1983, pp. 19-23.

8.  See for instance, A. Joseph Dowd and John R. Burton, "Deregulation Is Not an Answer for Electric Utilities," Public Utilities Fortnightly, Sept. 16, 1982, pp. 21-28.

9.  See for instance, Alvin Kaufman and Karen Nelson, "Deregulation and Reregulation of the Electric Utility Industry," Issue Brief No. IB83109, Congressional Research Service, June 17, 1983.

10. Irwin M. Stelzer, "Electric Utilities—Next Stop for Deregulators?," Regulation, July/August 1982, p. 35.

11. Stanley York, conversation with author, May 23, 1983.

12. Chris Warner, presentation at electricity regulation seminar, Government Institutes Inc., Washington, D.C., March 3, 1983.

13. Robert Spann, conversation with author, July 6, 1983.

14. Peter Navarro, "Our Stake in the Electric Utility's Dilemma," Harvard Business Review, May-June 1982, p. 97.

15. Chris Warner, op. cit.

16. National Governors' Association, op. cit., p. 12.

17. Ibid., p. 12.

18. See Mason Willrich and Kermit Kubitz, "Why Not Regional Electric Power Generation Companies," Public Utilities Fortnightly, June 9, 1983, p. 25.

19. "The Movement to Revise the Public Utility Holding Company Act: An Update," Public Utilities Fortnightly, Dec. 8, 1983, p. 39.

20. National Governors' Association, op. cit.

21. Edward Helme, presentation at electricity regulation seminar, Government Institutes Inc., Washington, D.C., March 3, 1983.

22. J. Robert Malko, interview with author, May 23, 1983.

# VI
# SUMMARY AND CONCLUSIONS

Energy issues continue to have a profound impact on many sectors of U.S. society. The electric utility industry, in particular, stands at the center of conflicting concerns about economic growth and employment, social welfare, the quality of the environment and national security. Many government and industry planners see abundant electricity supplies as a key resource in efforts to revitalize the U.S. economy and achieve sustained economic growth. But consumers are angry with rapidly rising electric bills, Wall Street is dismayed over the financial consequences of nuclear plant delays and cancellations, and scientists warn of the heavy environmental costs associated with nuclear and coal-fired power plants. Thus, the industry has found itself embroiled in an increasingly polarized and politicized debate over its proper role in the energy economy and its vision of the future. The debate is unlikely to be resolved soon and its outcome will have enormous ramifications for many sectors of the economy.

Pressures: A raft of economic pressures that began with the Arab oil embargo a decade ago has significantly damaged the financial position of electric utilities. High inflation, soaring operating and construction costs, stagnant electricity demand growth and lagging technological innovation have exacted an awesome toll on the nation's most capital-intensive industry, transforming it from a decreasing cost to an increasing cost business. Some of these pressures were easing slightly as the industry entered 1984. But a new set of economic pressures, such as increased competition within the industry and competition from other energy service companies, appeared to be taking hold. At the same time, ballooning political pressures stemming from increased regulation and the growing politicization of the utility decisionmaking process have further sapped the industry's vitality and financial strength. Regulators, ratepayers, stockholders, the financial community and special interest groups have all managed

to increase their influence on the utility planning process at the expense of utility managers. Together, these forces have combined to
make electric utilities a relatively poor investment over the last
decade. Moreover, it is becoming increasingly apparent that many of
these pressures are structural in nature, not temporary, which suggests that the industry is unlikely to undergo the kind of dramatic
cyclical recovery that many Wall Street analysts are predicting.

New management strategies: The economic and political pressures
facing the industry are forcing electric utilities to reexamine every
aspect of their businesses. As utility executives struggle to adapt to
the industry's changed business environment, they are increasingly
questioning many of the basic premises that have long guided utility
planning. Their actions show a growing realization that regulatory
changes of the magnitude needed to reverse the industry's weak
financial situation are unlikely and that new management approaches
will be needed if the industry is to remain viable through the re-
mainder of the century.

Several significant trends are emerging that appear to be common to virtually all utilities, including the use of new financing
techniques, adjustments in pricing and marketing strategies and the
adoption of stringent cost control programs. Beyond this, however,
the traditional consensus within the industry as to the proper basic
business strategy is breaking down as utilities begin to experiment
with various alternative business strategies. The so-called grow and
build strategy that virtually the entire industry followed since its
inception is giving way to new ideas. While it is clear that many
utilities have not yet defined any clear course of action for the
future, at least four major strategic paths can be seen emerging
among industry leaders: a modified grow and build strategy, a capital
minimization strategy, a renewable energy supply strategy and a
diversification strategy.

Utilities pursuing a modified grow and build strategy are continuing to emphasize the construction of large central-station generating plants to meet an anticipated rebound in electricity demand
growth. Many of these utilities are involved in massive nuclear and
coal plant construction programs begun in the 1970s and remain convinced that finishing those programs is their best option--even if it
entails larger immediate rate increases for their customers and continuing dilution of shareholders equity resulting from heavy financing
requirements. To counter some of the problems engendered by this
strategy, many utilities following this course have beefed up their
public relations efforts, stretched out plant construction schedules
and shifted future planning away from new nuclear plant construction
toward the use of conventional and advanced coal technologies. In
explaining the rationale for their strategy, these utilities stress the
possibility of power shortages later in the decade if construction
programs are cut back, emphasize the need to displace existing oil-
and gas-fired generating capacity, cite the unique importance of

electricity to the continued development of productivity-improving industries such as computers and robotics, and argue that overzealous regulatory requirements are primarily responsible for the cost increases now afflicting the industry.

Another group of utilities has reacted to the uncertainties facing the industry by adopting a capital minimization strategy designed to reduce corporate and shareholder risks until the proper course of action becomes more clear. These utilities are taking a number of actions to minimize current capital expenditures, including canceling plants under construction, selling existing generating capacity, undertaking programs to upgrade and extend the useful life of existing capacity, implementing serious conservation and load management programs, entering into regional or joint ownership agreements with other utilities and signing contracts to purchase power from other utilities and small power producers. For some, the reasoning behind adoption of this strategy is simple—it was the strategy that offered the best prospect for corporate survival. For a number of other utilities, however, including some that are in very good financial shape relative to the rest of .the industry, capital minimization is seen as the logical response to the uncertainties of the current economic and regulatory climate.

A renewable energy supply strategy is being adopted by two major utilities in California and seems likely to gain additional adherents among utilities with rapidly growing service territories or with regulatory climates that discourage nuclear and coal plant construction. Among the most significant elements of this strategy are an emphasis on the use of renewable energy sources, expanded research and development efforts, a focus on the addition of small, modular units of capacity and the use of long-term purchase contracts with outside entrepreneurs. The utilities pursuing this strategy explain it in terms of a strategy that provides greater flexibility in meeting changes in demand, technology and regulatory requirements while reducing financial risks. In addition, they see economic and public relations advantages in a shift to renewables because of the increasing cost of finding and extracting non-renewable fuels, the cost and image problems plaguing nuclear power development, the growing concerns with the environmental consequences of burning coal and the rapidly falling cost curves associated with many renewable technologies.

A final group of utilities is pursuing a diversification strategy aimed at investing cash flow in faster growing, more profitable ventures outside of the electric utility business. While many utilities are exploring new business ventures on a small scale, only a few have diversified to the extent that these ventures comprise a significant portion of their total business. Electric utility diversification efforts are occurring in areas such as oil and gas exploration, coal mining, energy and engineering services, real estate, aquaculture, telecommunications, and computer and financial services. The regulatory response to utility diversification efforts has been fragmented, and the industry's diversification moves are resulting in the creation of a number of different organizational structures within the industry. The utilities pursuing diversification see it as a means of escaping regulation and the inadequate returns available in the electric power business, avoiding the risks of being confined to a capital-intensive industry with dim growth prospects, and attracting new investor interest and capital.

Proposed regulatory changes: As the pressures on many segments of the electric power industry have mounted, they have inevitably brought forth calls for regulatory reform as a means of coping with some of the industry's problems. A number of proposals for structural reform of electric power regulation have been put forth. These proposals can be grouped into four major categories: those aimed at deregulating certain segments of the industry or certain types of power transactions; proposals for total or partial federal preemption of states' ratemaking authority; proposals for the regionalization of power planning or rate regulation; and proposals for greater public ownership of the industry.

Elements from a number of these proposals have economic merit and are being implemented on an ad hoc or experimental basis in various parts of the country. Nevertheless, the political hurdles confronting any proposal for major structural changes in the existing utility regulatory system are considerable. The Reagan administration will be particularly inhibited in its options for proposing changes in electric power regulation by its states' rights orientation.

Comprehensive deregulation appears exceedingly unlikely in the short term in view of the prodigious economic and legal obstacles to vertical disintegration in the industry and the lack of a clear constituency in favor of this approach. Federal preemption would face enormous opposition from the states and would be anathema to the Reagan administration. Regionalization might be acceptable to the Reagan administration but would still face considerable oppostion from the states and consumers. Finally, although public power is likely to continue to chip away at the investor-owned segment of the industry in some regions, there is little congressional support for the concept of total public ownership of the utility industry--a move perceived as a step toward socialism.

Congressional tinkering with the industry's existing regulatory system will undoubtedly continue over the next several years, but such changes seem destined to have little impact on the fundamental problems facing the industry. Later, more drastic regulatory changes--particularly moves toward deregulation--may gain political support as a result of the emergence of a whole new industry of energy service companies that operate in a deregulated environment. Technological advances such as the proliferation of microprocessors will also enhance the prospects for price deregulation in the longer term.

The most important near term regulatory changes from an investor standpoint may come at the state level in the form of greater cooperation between utility and regulatory planning staffs. Tough, well-funded regulatory staffs that are actively involved in the utility planning process appear to be associated with aggressive, well-managed utilities--although this phenomenon is contrary to conventional wisdom. Overall, regulatory changes will only accelerate the rate at which competitive elements are introduced into electricity markets, and thus they cannot be expected to alleviate the financial problems of much of the industry.

Implications: The diverse business strategies now being pursued by electric utilities are based on widely varying perceptions of the business environment the industry is likely to face over the next decade and beyond. Numerous uncertainties still face all utility planners, but many now have sufficient conviction in their visions of the future that they are choosing to assume significant risks to position their companies. Because utilities are following such different strategies and have such dichotomous views about the future, there are likely to be some big winners and some big losers in the industry--a dramatic contrast to the staid homogeneity that has characterized it in the past. Thus, the structure of industry will change much more rapidly in the next decade than it has in the past as a shakeout occurs among companies that have positioned themselves incorrectly. Well managed utilities with successful strategies are likely to become "cash cows" with sufficient funds to undertake large R&D programs to develop new generating technologies or to enter new businesses. A number of poorly managed utilities, or those with poor strategic plans, are likely to face reorganization or bankruptcy.

It remains somewhat premature to predict which utility business strategies will produce the winners and the losers, but predicting the relative performance of the various strategies under alternative economic and political scenarios would appear to be relatively straightforward.

Modified grow and build strategy--For the grow and build strategy to be successful, a relatively lengthy period of vigorous economic growth and low inflation is necessary, accompanied by the continuing substitution of electricity for other forms of energy. Under this kind of an economic environment, it is conceivable that utilities pursuing a grow and build strategy could increase their electricity sales substantially at the expense of other utilities that did not undertake expansion programs that were adequate to meet the growth in demand. Domestically, the early and widespread use of electric cars and trains--if it were to occur--would help bolster demand for centrally generated electric power. Internationally, greater instability of oil supplies from the Middle East or another round of large price increases would encourage greater reliance on domestic sources of energy, including electricity, although the adverse consequences of large oil price increases for economic growth might offset much of the need for additional electric power supplies.

Conversely, a prolonged continuation of weak overall economic growth or a reversal of the trend toward consumer substitution from other forms of energy toward electricity would be disastrous for companies pursuing the grow and build strategy. Equally disastrous for these companies would be confirmation that the electric power industry is a fully mature industry, with stable or declining demand. Rapid technological advances and commercialization of decentralized electricity sources such as solar power, wind energy and industrial cogeneration systems would also have negative implications for utilities building new nuclear and coal-fired plants, as would major declines in the relative price of alternative fuels. A prolonged collapse of world oil prices, for instance, would make many of the nuclear and coal-fired plants now under construction economically obsolete before they were even completed. Finally, the rejection of nuclear or coal-based technologies for social or environmental reasons continues to pose a credible threat to the ultimate success of any utility relying on these technologies. Public tolerance of nuclear generating plants is extremely fragile and remains subject to the safe operation of these plants around the world. Similarly, growing public concerns with the environmental consequences of burning coal—especially such intractable problems as acid rain, carbon dioxide buildup and shortages of water in the West--promise to spur more debate and legislation in these areas.

Capital minimization strategy--The ultimate success of companies following a capital minimization strategy is highly dependent on their individual circumstances as well as trends in the economy. For companies with an abundance of surplus low-cost generating capacity and slowly growing service territories, the capital minimization strategy would appear to offer the prospect of several years' respite from the financing problems, large rate increases and strategic dilemmas facing most of the industry. This will be true regardless of the strength and duration of the U.S. economic recovery. These companies are also likely to be among the best performers in the industry under a slow growth economic scenario. Thus, for these companies anyway, capital minimization is an inherently less risky strategy in the short run than the other three strategies. During this period, utilities pursuing this strategy will have the opportunity to survey the successes and failures of utilities adopting more aggressive business strategies before making any major strategic decisions. They will also have more time and more funds to assess new technological and political developments affecting the relative economic prospects of various generating technologies before committing themselves to new capital projects. This could prove to be extremely advantageous if there are major technological breakthroughs in the industry in the next few years or if environmental or political events dictate a switch away from new nuclear or coal-based generating plants.

The capital minimization strategy is not without its risks, of course. Companies following this strategy clearly run the risk of falling behind on the technological front if they do not aggressively fund their R&D efforts. Other companies may gain an advantage from their experience with building or operating state-of-the-art power plants or from their early involvement in non-utility business ventures. Moreover, once the cloud of uncertainty now hanging over the industry clears, it is almost inevitable that the utilities now minimizing their capital expenditures will be playing catchup with the utilities following at least one of the other three strategies. Finally, not all utilities that have adopted a capital minimization strategy have a large surplus of relatively inexpensive generating capacity. Some have relatively modest reserve margins and run the risk of being caught short of capacity in the event of a brisk economic recovery. Others have large percentages of oil- or gas-fired capacity, making them heavily dependent on the vagaries of the world oil market and legislation affecting natural gas prices.

Renewable energy supply strategy--Companies pursuing a renewable energy supply strategy appear to face a somewhat unique set of potential rewards. Politically and environmentally, this strategy appears to have a number of important advantages. Public support for utilities pursuing this strategy is greater than for utilities pushing nuclear and coal-based systems, potential legal and environmental costs will be reduced, and state regulatory commission support for these projects is likely to be higher. From an economic standpoint, the modular nature of most renewable technologies promises to offer much greater flexibility in meeting changing load forecasts and cost estimates than do conventional power plants. Meanwhile, the smaller size and shorter licensing and construction times associated with renewables will translate into tangible economic advantages--including lower financing costs and the option of allowing third parties to supply most of the capital and take most of the risks involved in new plant construction. Finally, the lack of fuel costs characteristic of many renewable energy sources means that once these units are installed they will be relatively impervious to energy supply disruptions or to fluctuations in fossil fuel prices or the rate of inflation.

Renewable technologies tend to be very capital-intensive. Thus if utilities actually try to build and own most of these generating units themselves, they will be taking some of the same risks as other growth oriented utilities. Companies taking the renewable route will clearly face some of the same risks regarding growth in the economy and the price of alternative fuels as utilities pursuing a grow and build strategy, although the diversification of energy sources and flexibility inherent in the renewables strategy appear to reduce the magnitude of these risks. These companies also face the possibility of investing in a number of generating technologies that will eventually prove to be unreliable, technologically immature or uneconomic. The operating lives of large wind turbines and of geothermal plants dependent on hot brine reservoirs, for instance, remain uncertain, as do the reliability characteristics of utility systems that are heavily dependent on energy sources such as solar and wind, which are hostage to local weather conditions. In addition, companies following this strategy could be hurt by the Reagan administration's ongoing efforts to end tax incentives and cut back research support for renewable energy development. Finally, utilities pursuing a strategy based on renewables ultimately confront the risk that their efforts to commercialize small, decentralized generating technologies will be too successful, leading to cost reductions of a magnitude sufficient to induce consumers to buy these generating sources for themselves and bypass electric utilities altogether.

Diversification strategy--The major advantages and disadvantages of the diversification strategy are clearly extremely dependent on the individual circumstances and opportunities of the companies involved. For some utilities, diversification outside of the electric utility industry appears to offer the prospect of less regulatory involvement and the chance to participate in some of the more dynamic and faster growing segments of the economy such as telecommunications, financial services, data processing and cable communications systems. For other utilities, diversification into other businesses seems to make sense based on scale economies or on the synergistic advantages that would accrue to a utility's operations or to the business being acquired. Strategic planning considerations also support efforts by electric utilities to broaden their business mix beyond the slow growth, extremely capital-intensive business of generating and distributing electric power. Utilities that are successful in developing or acquiring businesses with superior profitability or growth potential will also enjoy additional benefits in the form of lower financing costs. In general, reorganization under a holding company structure appears to offer utilities the prospect of greater financial and business flexibility. Overall, it is difficult to generalize about the performance of utilities that pursue diversification because of the plethora of new businesses that utilities are entering. Diversified utilities are likely to outperform undiversified electric utilities, however, if the industry has entered a no growth or declining phase.

The major risks involved in the diversification strategy include both the economic risks that accompany any company's efforts to expand into new business areas and the risk that regulatory authorities will seek to exercise some form of control over unregulated utility subsidiaries. The economic risks of utility diversification have gained increased attention recently, primarily because the majority of existing utility ventures are in energy-related businesses that have been hit hard by cyclical and structural changes in world energy markets. There are also growing concerns among many analysts, however, about whether the management styles and philosophies typical of many electric utilities will be capable of handling business operations in unregulated markets and about whether already cash-strapped utilities will have the necessary funds to undertake significant diversification programs. Meanwhile, the issue of how the earnings of unregulated utility subsidiaries will be treated by regulators, especially during a period when ratepayer anger is growing over rapidly rising electric rates, continues to cast a cloud over the future of utility diversification efforts. Many observers believe that state utility commissions will feel extreme pressure to find ways to use unregulated earnings to help moderate rate increases even if the new ventures were started entirely with stockholder money.

Outlook: The electric utility industry has entered a critical transition period in its development that will result in significant structural changes in the industry and major strategic changes among utilities over the next decade. There are strong indications that the electric utility industry is now maturing. Whether and when the industry will enter the declining phase that some mature industries undergo remains open to question. In any case, this transition period will create enormous difficulties for some electric utilities. In the near term, the severe financial difficulties encountered recently by several utilities with nuclear plants under construction are likely to continue and such problems are likely to spread to a number of other utilities that are pushing forward with attempts to complete reactor projects. The inexorable movement away from nuclear power that these financial problems portend, however, will not solve some of the more fundamental dilemmas facing the industry. Over the longer term, the real challenge to utility managements will come as the monopoly status of the industry is eroded by competition with other utilities and energy sources and with companies marketing energy services. The precursors of these longer term transitional problems are already becoming apparent in the form of large rate increases, lack of growth in electricity demand, increased public opposition to the use of nuclear and coal-fired generating plants and deterioration in the industry's financial condition.

At the same time, electricity remains essential to the information-related and service industries that are coming to dominate the U.S. economy. For existing utilities that properly adjust their business strategies to the economic realities, the transition phase could provide opportunities for strengthening the balance sheet and defining market niches that can be served profitably. Moreover, for companies that manage to maintain financial strength and flexibility, the changing economic and regulatory climate that utilities face appears to offer immense new business opportunities to utilities over the longer term, provided they can capitalize on their inherent strengths in the areas of engineering, customer service and finance. Historically, the companies in other maturing industries that have been most successful at managing their way through the transition period have also been major participants in the successor or substitute industry. Thus, while uncertainties abound concerning the companies best positioned for this future, current evidence suggests that the utilities most likely to prosper are those that are aggressively adapting to the industry's new environment through the pursuit of strategies that limit the need for and risks of new plant construction, allow diversification into other business areas and access to new financing mechanisms, and shift corporate resources away from obsolete technologies toward the cleaner, more efficient generating technologies and energy services now being developed.

# APPENDICES

## APPENDIX A

# New business ventures: What 79 investor-owned electric utilities are doing

| Utility | Ventures | Remarks |
|---|---|---|
| Alabama Power Co | Coal reserve holdings; cogeneration projects; district heating; real estate services; appliance sales and service; assured heat-pump service program; Centsable action program | Centsable Action program provides free audits, promotes insulation and installation of heat-recovery units on heat pumps. |
| American Electric Power Service Corp | Coal affiliates | Subsidiary coal companies owned directly by Ohio Power, Appalachian Power, and Indiana & Michigan Electric. Annual production, about 14-million tons. |
| Arizona Public Service Co | Bixco Inc; Energy Development Co; Resources Co: uranium exploration and development | Bixco subsidiary is in gas exploration and development. Energy Development Co subsidiary's activities include residential and industrial construction, real-estate investments, energy-conservation installations, chilled-water service for shopping malls, etc, and short-line railroad and hotel/resort development. Resources Co subsidiary is concerned with coal reserves. Uranium activities are being disbanded. |
| Arkansas Power & Light Co | Low-grade thermal solar project; District-heating and -cooling project; thermal-storage project; central Arkansas cogeneration project; south Arkansas cogeneration project; conservation financing plan; irrigation switches; air-conditioner switches | Cogeneration projects include coal gasification of Illinois coal, as well as petroleum coke, to produce medium-Btu gas to be pipelined to combined-cycle cogeneration plants located near industries requiring process steam in central and southern Arkansas. |
| Atlantic City Electric Co | DuPont cogeneration agreements | Utility has installed boilers and generating equipment to supply process steam, water, and byproduct electricity to DuPont at two locations. |

|  | | |
|---|---|---|
| Baltimore Gas & Electric Co | District heating; appliance merchandising and service | Utility customer-service department services all appliances company sells, including air conditioners, dishwashers, and television and sound equipment. |
| Bangor Hydro-Electric Co | East Branch Improvement Co | Joint venture with Great Northern Paper Co to own and operate water-storage dams. |
| Black Hills Power & Light Co | Subsidiary Coal Co | Subsidiary supplies coal to company-owned plants. |
| Boston Edison Co | RESCO | Cogeneration of steam and electricity from urban refuse. A subsidiary. |
| Carolina Power & Light Co | Leslie & McInnes coal-mining companies | CP&L owns 80% of outstanding shares of stock in these subsidiary coal mines. Gets corresponding share of coal produced. |
| Central & South West Corp | Central & South West Fuels | Subsidiary responsible for certain nonpetroleum power activities. |
| Central Maine Power Co | Central Securities Corp; Cumberland Securities Corp; Union Water Power Co | Real-estate investments and water storage. All subsidiaries. |
| Central Power & Light Co | Joint venture with Haas, McNeil & Wilson | Oil and gas exploration and development. |
| Central Vermont Public Service Corp | Rental water-heater program | Rental of 24,000 electric water heaters. Goal: Provide service and a return on investment in excess of what is allowed by regulation. |
| Cleveland Electric Illuminating Co | Real estate | Buy real estate for company needs and limited industrial-development services. |
| Commonwealth Edison Co | Cotter Corp; Edison Development Co; Edison Development Canada, Inc | Subsidiaries are responsible for acquisition, development, and production of coal and uranium reserves. |

| Utility | Ventures | Remarks |
| --- | --- | --- |
| Consolidated Edison Co of NY | Blue-ribbon service; solar water heating; energy-conservation homes; district heating | Blue-ribbon service inspects customers homes, recommends energy-conservation measures, and acts as general contractors to implement audit recommendations on request. |
| Consumers Power Co | Plateau Resources Ltd; Michigan Utility Collection Service Co, Inc; Northern Michigan Exploration Co; Michigan Gas Storage Co | Four subsidiaries are involved in uranium production, bill collections, oil-and-gas exploration, and interstate natural-gas operations. |
| Dayton Power & Light Co | Residential energy audits; residential energy services | Energy audits and feasibility studies on maintenance contracts for home-heating systems. Getting into appliance sales business. |
| Delmarva Power & Light Co | Industrial steam project | Supplies steam to industrial customers. |
| Detroit Edison Co | Nuclear-fuel supply; coal-fuel supply; coal transloading; aquaculture | Transloading facility for movement of low-sulfur coal from Montana to Michigan, and experimental aquaculture project. |
| Duke Power Co | Crescent Land & Timber Corp; The Eastover Companies; Mill-Power Supply Co; Western Fuel Inc; load management, appliance sales and service | Four subsidiaries involved in timber harvesting and reforestation, coal mining, electrical equipment wholesaling, and uranium resource development. |
| Duquesne Light Co. | Allegheny County Steam Heating Co | Subsidiary steam-heating service |
| El Paso Electric Co | Franklin Land & Resources Inc | Investments in plant site, uranium property, office buildings, parking lots, farms for water rights and cattle. A subsidiary. |
| Fitchburg Gas & Electric Light Co | Word-processing market; appliance leasing; residential energy audits; Fitchburg Energy Development Co; cogeneration; real-estate disposition | Energy Development Co subsidiary explores for and develops oil and natural-gas resources. Word-processing activity involves in-house company staff working overtime to provide word-processing service to business and industry in the company's service area. Real estate operation sells R-O-W land no longer needed. |

|  |  |
|---|---|
| Florida Power & Light Co | Fuel Supply Service Inc | Nuclear and fossil-fuel resource development and exploration. A subsidiary. |
| Florida Power Corp | Electric Fuels Corp | Subsidiary is involved in coal acquisition, sales, mining, marine transportation, R&D, and commercialization, as well as bulk materials-handling terminals and alternative-fuels development. |
| Georgia Power Co | Forest/land management; steam heat; ash management | Management of land holdings, steam sales, and flyash sales. |
| Green Mountain Power Co | Lease-Elec; energy thrift certificates | Subsidiary rents heat-storage equipment to consumers. Certificates are 360-day notes for minimum of $500, sold to state residents as alternative source of capital. |
| Gulf Power Co | Good Cents energy-conservation program; appliance sales and service | Energy-conservation services, and appliance sales and service. |
| Gulf States Utilities Co | Varibus Corp | Subsidiary is in fossil- and nuclear-fuel exploration and development as well as natural-gas pipelines. |
| Houston Industries Inc | Primary Fuels Inc; Utility Fuels Inc | Offshore oil and gas drilling for pipeline transmission and oil-company markets is done by first subsidiary; second is involved in coal mining, handling, and transportation, and uranium mining, for electric utilities, coal-gasification facilities, and other industries. |
| Idaho Power Co | Idaho Energy Resources Co | Subsidiary covers coal, uranium, and thorium. |
| Illinois Power Co | Illinois Power Fuel Co; aquaculture; and load management | 50%-owned affiliate finances purchase of nuclear fuel for Clinton power station. Aquaculture project features greenhouse heating demonstration at Baldwin station. |

| Utility | Ventures | Remarks |
| --- | --- | --- |
| Indianapolis Power & Light Co | District heating | Steam supply in Indianapolis. |
| Iowa Electric Light & Power Co | Railway transportation; real estate; co-generation | Short-line railway and real-estate acquisition subsidiaries. |
| Iowa Public Service Co | Cimmarina; aquaculture; load management: Energy Development Co | Subsidiary operates boat marina. Energy Development Co subsidiary is in surface and underground coal mining in Wyoming. |
| Iowa Resources Inc | Middlewood Inc; Unitrain Inc; Enercor Inc; Enserco Inc; Redlands Inc; Iowa Computer Resources Inc; Industries of Iowa Corp: Iowa Power Resources Inc | Eight subsidiaries own and develop real estate; manage, own, and lease unit trains; own coal lands; lease lands for farming and ranching; provide energy-related engineering construction and maintenance services to industries and utilities; sell internally developed computer software; are involved in ethyl alcohol plant and two grain alcohol plants; own gas pipeline; and explore and develop natural-gas reserves. |
| Iowa Southern Utilities | Unitrain Maintenance Co; Southern Iowa Manufacturing Co; appliance sales and service: conservation services | Unitrain subsidiary maintains rail cars. Southern Iowa subsidiary makes drilling equipment. |
| Kansas City Power & Light Co | WYMO Fuels Inc; district heating; real estate: waste product sales | Fuels subsidiary is waiting for permit to mine proposed 4-million ton/year of coal in Campbell County, Wyo. Utility also sells ash products through marketing brokers. |
| Long Island Lighting Co | Consumer energy seminars; solar water-heating program | Classroom instruction on practical and theoretical energy concerns. |
| Madison Gas & Electric Co | MAGAEL Inc; MG&E Nuclear Fuel Inc; MAGAEL Material Resources Inc | Three subsidiaries are involved in real estate, nuclear-fuel ownership, and acquisition uranium. |
| Middle South Utilities | System Fuels Inc | Subsidiary procures, stores, and transports fuels for MSU operating companies, and explores for oil, gas, and uranium. |

| | | |
|---|---|---|
| Mississippi Power & Light Co | Steam sales; cooking-equipment sales; electric water-heater sales; load management; energy services | Counterline commercial electric cooking equipment is sold to small restaurants in towns with no other distributors. |
| Montana-Dakota Utilities Co | Knife River Coal Mining Co; Fidelity Gas Co; appliance on sales and service | Two subsidiaries are involved in lignite surface-mining operations and oil and natural-gas leases. |
| Montana Power Co | Western Energy Co; Sunlight Development Co; Butte Aero; Canadian Montana Pipeline Co; Canadian Montana Gas Co, Roan Resources Ltd, Altana Exploration Co; North American Resources Co | Six subsidiaries are engaged in exploration, leasing, development, marketing, and operation of coal and lignite properties; sales of oil, natural gas, and other petroleum products in Canada and the United States; and management and development of commercial, industrial, agricultural, and recreational real estate, and home rentals and sales. Subsidiary Butte Aero is involved in aircraft sales and charters, student training, aircraft maintenance, and fuel sales. |
| Nevada Power Co | Load management; energy-conservation services | Radio-control system to cycle air-conditioning loads. |
| New England Electric System | New England Collier Co; New England Energy Inc; The Energy Institute; Two-Way Automatic Communication System (TWACS) | New England Collier subsidiary is a joint venture with Keystone Shipping Co to build and operate self-unloading coal collier chartered to New England Power Co; New England Energy subsidiary has 50% partnerships with established oil and gas exploration companies for on- and offshore drilling; Energy Institute provides seminars and workshops on conservation and load-management techniques for utility industry managers; TWACS is a technology for two-way communications over power lines. New England Power Service Co holds patent and has granted exclusive license to Emerson Electric Co for manufacture and sales. |

| Utility | Ventures | Remarks |
| --- | --- | --- |
| New England Gas & Electric Assn (Commonwealth Energy System) | Cambridge Steam Corp; NEGEA Energy Services Inc; Darvel Realty Trust; NEGEA Realty Trust | Subsidiaries are involved in resale steam, investment in gas and oil drilling, real-estate operations. |
| Niagara Mohawk Power Corp | NM Uranium Inc: energy-conservation services | Uranium subsidiary has 50% interest in southern Texas uranium mine. |
| Northeast Utilities Co | Conn Save | Subsidiary has 75% share of joint venture by Connecticut utilities to provide residential conservation services. Customers are charged $10 for audits; balance of costs are passed on to all-electric consumers. |
| Northern States Power Co | Energy-system services: thermal-energy sales; residential-energy programs; warm-water green-house service | Provides management services to other companies that use large energy systems; NSP provides 1600 gpm of warm water to commercial green-house operation. |
| Ohio Edison Co | District heating | District steam-heating systems in two cities. |
| Orange & Rockland Utilities | O&R Energy Development Inc | Subsidiary explores for gas and oil in southern Mississippi. |
| Otter Tail Power Co | Custom billing: real estate; materials testing. | Company's computers are used for billing of municipal services for nine communities. Real-estate operation is a subsidiary. |
| Pacific Gas & Electric Co | Energy-services training: oil-field cogeneration: methane-gas production; load management; Pacific Gas Transmission Co; Natural Gas Corp of California; Pacific Energy Services Corp; Eureka Energy Co | Cogeneration project uses hot turbine steam for injection into oil wells for enhanced recovery. Methane gas is produced from sanitary landfill and cattle-feedlot waste. Four subsidiaries are involved in gas transportation, and in exploration, acquisition, and development of coal and geothermal-resource properties. Pacific Energy Services Corp subsidiary is a planned venture to finance cost-effective conservation investments. |

Pacific Power & Light Co — Alascom Inc: Telephone Utilities Inc; NERCO Inc; water sales; district heating; Wyopac Service Inc Williamette Development Co — Alascom subsidiary operates long-line telecommunication and computer-data transmission service in Alaska. Other subsidiaries operate telephone companies in six states, coal-mining and uranium-exploration operations, retail water distribution, equipment-leasing operations, and real-estate development.

Pennsylvania Electric Co — Nineveh Water Co; steam heating — Water and steam (cogeneration) service.

Pennsylvania Power & Light Co — Pennsylvania Mines Corp; Arcadia Co; Interstate Energy Co; residential audits; aquaculture — Three subsidiaries are involved in coal mining, coal sales, and oil-pipeline transportation.

Philadelphia Electric Co — Adwin Realty Co; Adwin Equipment Co; Eastern Pennsylvania Exploration Co; Adex Display; appliance sales; R&D projects/engineering; Lee mine — Four subsidiaries are involved in real-estate development, equipment leasing, and operation of public shipping terminal, as well as gas exploration and drilling and a complete graphic-arts service. Company is also involved in joint venture with Kerr-McGee Nuclear Corp to develop new uranium mine near Grants, NM.

Public Service Co of Colorado — Fuel Resources Development Co; 1480 Welton Inc — Two subsidiaries are involved in natural-gas, oil, and coal supplies. Coal-mining company is inactive.

Public Service Co of New Mexico — Paragon Resources Inc; Sunbelt Mining Co; Western Coal Co — Three subsidiaries are involved in acquisition of water and property, coal supplies, and as crushed-stone and trucking operations.

Public Service Co of Oklahoma — Transok Pipe Line Co — Transok provides a firm supply of natural gas to PSO for use in generation. It also serves as PSO's agent in dealing with gas producers, and is fuel-oil purchasing agent for the parent company.

| Utility | Ventures | Remarks |
|---|---|---|
| Public Service Electric & Gas Co | Gasdel Pipeline System Inc; Energy Development Corp (EDC); Limestone Springs Fishing Preserve; Mercer Aquaculture Facility; coal-bed degasification; coal conversion; methane-gas production; waste-heat agriculture; district heating/cooling; contract R&D and architect/engineer services; quality-control and testing services | Coal-bed degasification, coal conversion, Gasdel, EDC, methane-gas production, and fishing preserve and aquaculture facility are subsidiaries. EDC is in oil and gas exploration. Quality control and testing services are a subsidiary operation, which does technical research and testing in metrology, sound level and vibration studies, chemical analysis, plant energy audits, and environmental studies. |
| Puget Sound Power & Light Co | Puget Sound Energy Co: energy-conservation services | Subsidiary is involved in oil and coal reserve development. Company provides interest-free loans for cost-effective residential modifications. |
| San Diego Gas & Electric Co | Japatul Corp; Applied Energy Inc; New Albion Resources Co | Three subsidiaries are involved in nonutility real-estate development, cogeneration, and coal, geothermal, oil, and gas exploration, development, and production. |
| Sierra Pacific Power Co | Sierra Energy Co; Lands of Sierra Inc | Two subsidiaries are involved in four-state natural-gas and oil exploration, and real-estate investment. |
| South Carolina Electric & Gas Co | South Carolina Fuel Co; South Carolina LNG Co; Energy Subsidiary Inc | Three subsidiaries were established to acquire fuel, and buy, sell, and invest in real estate. |
| Southern California Edison Co | Electric Systems Co (ESC); Orange County Energy Conservation Assn (OCECA); Energy Conservation Systems Inc (ECS); Energy Systems Inc (ESI); Southern Surplus Realty Co; Associated Southern Investment Co; Mono Power Co | Company subsidiaries (ECS and OCECA not included) were formed to enhance utility activities in load management, metering, alternative energy resources, and real-estate development. |
| Southwestern Electric Power Co | Arklahoma Corp | Joint venture with Arkansas Power & Light Co and Oklahoma Gas & Electric Co for gas exploration. |

Tampa Electric Co (TECO Energy Inc) — Electro-Coal Transfer Corp; Gulf Coast Transit Co; Mid-South Towing Co; Southern Marine Management Co; G.C. Service Co; Tampa Bay Industrial Corp; Cal-Glo Coal Inc — Seven subsidiaries are involved in coal transport by water, as well as other bulk products, coal mining, coal-unloading facilities, and city parking-lot operation.

Texas Utilities Co — Chaco Energy Co; Basic Resources Inc — Two subsidiaries were organized for coal-supply acquisition; oil, gas, and lignite exploration; and natural resource development.

Union Electric Co — Union Colliery Co; district heating — Colliery Co subsidiary owns coal reserves and real estate.

UGI Corp — Universal Well Services; IPSCO and Triad Drilling Co; Ashtola Production Co — Three subsidiaries are involved in well fractionation, contract drilling, and oil and gas production.

Virginia Electric & Power Co — Vepco commercial-paper operations; Laurel Run Mining Co; Project Information & Control System (PICS) — Mining company subsidiary provides coal supplies. Vepco markets commercial paper to prospective buyers and sells it for another utility on an "as agent" basis. PICS provides software, training, and specialized system development for engineering and construction firms and utilities for integration of planning and scheduling, cost management, and accounting.

Washington Water Power Co — Development Associates Inc; Washington Irrigation & Development Co; Water Power Improvement Co; Spokane Industrial Park Inc — Four subsidiaries are involved in oil, gas, and coal operations; R&D on portable billing system, and real-estate operations.

Wisconsin Electric Power Co — Badger Service Co; district heating — Subsidiary operates parking lots, holds coal rights.

Wisconsin Power & Light Co — NUFUS Resources Inc; ash sales; customer billing services; steam sales; appliance service; furnace modification; solar water-heating program — NUFUS subsidiary is involved in exploration and mining to supply nuclear fuel. Sale of vanadium is a byproduct.

Wisconsin Public Service Corp — Delores Bench Ltd partnership — Uranium mining and milling

## APPENDIX B

# Selected Financial Indicators - 1981

| Utilities | Capitalization Ratios¹ | | | | Rate of Return on Electric Utility Rate Base | Common Equity Percent of Total Capitalization² | Rate of Return on Common Equity | Interest Coverage Times Earned | |
|---|---|---|---|---|---|---|---|---|---|
| | Common Equity | Preferred Stock | Long-Term Debt | Short-Term Debt (Notes Payable) | | | | Before Taxes | After Taxes |
| **ALABAMA** | | | | | | | | | |
| Alabama Power Co. | 80.1 | 10.2 | 59.7 | .0 | 7.69 | 80.9 | 8.2 | 1.49 | 1.49 |
| Southern Electric Generating Co. | 41.8 | .0 | 58.2 | .0 | 8.03 | 41.4 | 15.4 | 4.50 | 2.55 |
| **ALASKA** | | | | | | | | | |
| Alaska Electric Light & Power Co. | 34.0 | 1.6 | 64.4 | .0 | 8.61 | 87.8 | 10.1 | 1.37 | 1.37 |
| **ARIZONA** | | | | | | | | | |
| Arizona Public Service Co. | 41.1 | 10.2 | 45.8 | 2.8 | 13.79 | 42.9 | 14.7 | 2.28 | 2.19 |
| Citizen Utilities Co. | 76.9 | .0 | 23.1 | .0 | 9.15 | 75.2 | 14.7 | 7.43 | 6.50 |
| Tucson Electric Power Co. | 36.9 | 7.6 | 55.4 | .0 | 8.63 | 38.4 | 22.0 | 2.09 | 2.09 |
| **ARKANSAS** | | | | | | | | | |
| Arkansas Power & Light Co. | 31.2 | 14.1 | 51.8 | 2.9 | 8.56 | 31.2 | 12.7 | 1.96 | 1.89 |
| **CALIFORNIA** | | | | | | | | | |
| Pacific Gas & Electric Co. | 37.1 | 14.2 | 41.6 | 7.1 | 7.92 | 40.3 | 11.4 | 2.35 | 2.21 |
| San Diego Gas & Electric Co. | 36.6 | 18.4 | 42.6 | 7.4 | 9.71 | 38.9 | 14.5 | 1.99 | 1.99 |
| Southern California Edison Co. | 38.5 | 11.4 | 46.3 | 3.8 | 9.71 | 39.5 | 15.3 | 2.63 | 2.46 |
| **COLORADO** | | | | | | | | | |
| Home Light & Power Co. | 58.8 | .0 | 34.6 | 6.6 | 9.15 | 61.4 | 10.6 | 3.08 | 2.30 |
| Public Service Co. of Colorado | 39.5 | 12.3 | 45.7 | 2.4 | 7.65 | 39.9 | 12.1 | 2.91 | 2.57 |
| **CONNECTICUT** | | | | | | | | | |
| Connecticut Light & Power Co. | 30.5 | 10.6 | 53.8 | 5.2 | 8.14 | 33.1 | 9.3 | 1.61 | 1.61 |
| Connecticut Yankee Atomic Power Co. | 38.4 | .0 | 46.3 | 15.8 | 5.76 | 44.9 | 14.3 | 1.28 | 1.44 |
| Hartford Electric Light Co., The | 31.0 | 12.4 | 46.7 | 9.9 | 8.90 | 35.2 | 10.7 | 1.80 | 1.76 |
| Northeast Nuclear Energy Co. | 36.1 | .0 | 36.5 | 27.4 | 4.78 | 48.0 | 14.3 | 1.84 | 1.31 |
| United Illuminating Co., The | 35.4 | 18.2 | 41.0 | 5.4 | 8.05 | 36.4 | 15.3 | 3.12 | 2.67 |
| **DELAWARE** | | | | | | | | | |
| Delmarva Power & Light Co. & Suba. Cos. | 36.8 | 13.0 | 50.2 | .0 | 8.55 | 36.1 | 11.0 | 2.31 | 2.04 |
| **DISTRICT OF COLUMBIA** | | | | | | | | | |
| Potomac Electric Power Co. | 37.3 | 10.7 | 45.9 | 6.1 | 8.95 | 38.7 | 12.4 | 2.59 | 2.31 |

| | | | | | | | | | |
|---|---|---|---|---|---|---|---|---|---|
| **FLORIDA** | | | | | | | | | |
| Florida Power Corp. | 34.5 | 11.5 | 52.4 | 1.5 | 8.61 | 34.6 | 15.0 | 2.44 | 2.26 |
| Florida Power & Light Co. | 35.3 | 3.2 | 51.7 | 3.8 | 8.63 | 37.0 | 12.0 | 2.09 | 1.91 |
| Florida Public Utilities Co. | 46.7 | 4.9 | 39.5 | 8.9 | 9.39 | 50.1 | 12.0 | 2.80 | 2.17 |
| Gulf Power Co. | 38.6 | 11.9 | 54.6 | .0 | 8.78 | 33.2 | 11.4 | 2.35 | 2.01 |
| Reedy Creek Utilities Co. | 70.2 | .0 | 29.8 | .0 | 4.94 | 69.8 | 4.2 | 2.49 | 2.22 |
| Tampa Electric Co. | 39.4 | 7.0 | 43.3 | 9.9 | 8.48 | 43.7 | 14.6 | 3.18 | 2.36 |
| **GEORGIA** | | | | | | | | | |
| Georgia Power Co. | 31.4 | 10.7 | 57.3 | .0 | 7.31 | 31.7 | 12.4 | 2.06 | 1.99 |
| Savannah Electric & Power Co. | 29.1 | 6.9 | 60.4 | 3.7 | 9.58 | 29.5 | 13.5 | 1.74 | 1.66 |
| **HAWAII** | | | | | | | | | |
| Hawaiian Electric Co., The | 41.6 | 10.2 | 42.7 | 5.4 | 9.88 | 42.7 | 12.5 | 2.64 | 2.12 |
| Hawaii Electric Light Co. | 35.6 | 11.5 | 52.9 | .0 | 7.63 | 35.9 | 10.2 | 2.14 | 1.84 |
| Maui Electric Co., Ltd. | 35.4 | 12.4 | 52.3 | .0 | 6.66 | 36.7 | 1.7 | 0.79 | 0.79 |
| **IDAHO** | | | | | | | | | |
| Idaho Power Co. | 34.0 | 10.1 | 50.1 | 5.8 | 8.06 | 36.9 | 10.8 | 1.83 | 1.78 |
| **ILLINOIS** | | | | | | | | | |
| Central Illinois Light Co. | 36.2 | 18.7 | 45.0 | 5.2 | 7.38 | 37.0 | 12.2 | 3.03 | 2.87 |
| Central Illinois Public Service Co. | 38.7 | 11.7 | 47.3 | 2.3 | 7.04 | 38.8 | 12.3 | 2.66 | 2.47 |
| Commonwealth Edison Co. | 31.7 | 10.8 | 51.5 | 6.0 | 8.55 | 38.5 | 11.5 | 1.86 | 1.83 |
| Electric Energy, Inc. | 32.6 | .0 | 28.6 | 38.8 | 9.60 | 49.7 | 13.0 | 1.69 | 1.37 |
| Illinois Power Co. | 39.6 | 11.5 | 45.7 | 3.2 | 10.26 | 39.4 | 13.3 | 2.70 | 2.46 |
| Mt. Carmel Public Utility Co. | 73.6 | 18.2 | 13.2 | .0 | 5.46 | 72.8 | 4.2 | 2.90 | 2.47 |
| Sherrard Power System | 47.1 | 6.4 | 40.5 | 6.1 | 6.87 | 52.1 | 4.6 | 1.72 | 1.60 |
| So. Beloit Water Gas & Elec. Co. | 100.0 | .0 | .0 | .0 | 24.33 | 100.0 | 6.7 | 24.54 | 81.19 |
| **INDIANA** | | | | | | | | | |
| Alcoa Generating Corp. | 100.0 | .0 | 0 | .0 | 1.52 | 100.0 | 1.6 | .00 | .00 |
| Commonwealth Edison Co., Inc. | 37.6 | 28.9 | 33.5 | .0 | 7.58 | 37.9 | 12.9 | 5.86 | 3.66 |
| Indiana Kentucky Electric Corp. | 4.2 | .0 | 95.8 | .0 | 1.70 | 3.4 | .0 | 1.06 | 1.03 |
| Indiana & Michigan Electric Co. | 32.3 | 11.8 | 53.9 | 2.1 | 9.34 | 33.1 | 10.1 | 1.75 | 1.70 |
| Indianapolis Power & Light Co. | 40.0 | 10.6 | 47.5 | 1.9 | 7.85 | 39.8 | 11.4 | 2.49 | 2.14 |
| No. Indiana Public Service Co. | 33.6 | 10.9 | 52.6 | 2.9 | 6.90 | 35.3 | 7.9 | 1.63 | 1.63 |
| Public Service Co. of Indiana, Inc. | 40.1 | 11.9 | 47.6 | 0.4 | 8.95 | 40.2 | 18.7 | 2.38 | 2.29 |
| So. Indiana Gas & Electric Co. | 39.9 | 10.1 | 50.0 | .0 | 7.89 | 41.7 | 13.8 | 3.65 | 2.69 |
| **IOWA** | | | | | | | | | |
| Interstate Power Co. | 36.0 | 11.7 | 52.3 | .0 | 8.13 | 35.6 | 11.2 | 3.27 | 2.31 |
| Iowa Electric Light & Power Co. | 34.0 | 12.3 | 47.0 | 6.7 | 7.66 | 36.1 | 11.5 | 1.91 | 1.91 |
| Iowa Illinois Gas & Electric Co. | 34.6 | 14.2 | 46.5 | 4.7 | 8.59 | 37.2 | 15.5 | 2.76 | 2.43 |
| Iowa Power & Light Co. | 28.4 | 8.6 | 58.5 | 4.5 | 8.74 | 28.8 | 14.0 | 2.25 | 2.16 |
| Iowa Public Service Co. | 35.1 | 11.3 | 58.7 | .0 | 8.88 | 35.6 | 11.5 | 2.32 | 2.03 |
| Iowa Southern Utilities Co. | 40.1 | 7.6 | 52.3 | .0 | 9.24 | 40.6 | 13.0 | 2.33 | 2.10 |
| **KANSAS** | | | | | | | | | |
| Central Telephone & Utilities Corp. | 69.8 | 2.9 | 27.8 | .0 | 7.20 | 69.6 | 17.8 | 5.78 | 5.78 |
| Kansas Gas & Electric Co. | 38.6 | 12.5 | 53.4 | 0.4 | 9.27 | 35.3 | 14.5 | 2.24 | 2.18 |
| Kansas Power & Light Co. | 42.5 | 11.4 | 43.0 | 3.0 | 8.87 | 42.1 | 13.7 | 3.10 | 2.86 |

# Selected Financial Indicators—Continued

| Utilities | Capitalization Ratios[1] | | | | Rate of Return on Electric Utility Rate Base | Common Equity Percent of Total Capitalization[2] | Rate of Return on Common Equity | Interest Coverage Times Earned | |
|---|---|---|---|---|---|---|---|---|---|
| | Common Equity | Preferred Stock | Long-Term Debt | Short-Term Debt (Notes Payable) | | | | Before Taxes | After Taxes |
| **KENTUCKY** | | | | | | | | | |
| Kentucky Power Co. | 38.6 | .0 | 53.1 | 8.3 | 8.20 | 42.7 | 9.47 | 1.66 | 1.60 |
| Kentucky Utilities Co. | 35.1 | 11.5 | 53.0 | 0.4 | 10.50 | 34.4 | 9.7 | 1.87 | 1.72 |
| Louisville Gas & Electric Co. | 35.8 | 12.8 | 44.9 | 6.5 | 10.42 | 37.7 | 11.2 | 2.61 | 2.33 |
| Union Light Heat & Power Co. | 49.2 | .0 | 50.8 | .0 | 6.08 | 51.8 | 4.7 | 1.66 | 1.66 |
| **LOUISIANA** | | | | | | | | | |
| Central Louisiana Electric Co., Inc. | 36.5 | 6.8 | 56.7 | .0 | 11.73 | 34.4 | 15.3 | 2.02 | 1.81 |
| Gulf States Utilities Co. | 33.2 | 11.1 | 54.5 | 1.2 | 14.36 | 32.7 | 14.2 | 1.97 | 1.90 |
| Louisiana Power & Light Co. | 31.8 | 14.2 | 51.6 | 2.9 | 15.92 | 32.3 | 16.5 | 2.47 | 2.25 |
| New Orleans Public Service, Inc. | 30.2 | 16.1 | 54.8 | .0 | 6.83 | 30.6 | 10.2 | 2.71 | 2.02 |
| **MAINE** | | | | | | | | | |
| Bangor Hydro-Electric Co. | 30.0 | 9.1 | 48.9 | 12.0 | 6.95 | 36.3 | 10.8 | 1.88 | 1.59 |
| Central Maine Power Co. | 35.8 | 12.8 | 48.2 | 3.2 | 9.22 | 37.8 | 10.5 | 1.84 | 1.84 |
| Maine Electric Power Co., Inc. | 10.4 | .0 | 89.6 | .0 | 8.95 | 10.2 | 12.1 | 1.16 | 1.12 |
| Maine Public Service Co. | 31.9 | 9.1 | 37.9 | 21.1 | 10.07 | 39.3 | 14.0 | 1.83 | 1.78 |
| Maine Yankee Atomic Power Co. | 30.1 | 5.8 | 59.8 | 4.3 | 3.51 | 31.0 | 10.2 | 1.64 | 1.43 |
| **MARYLAND** | | | | | | | | | |
| Baltimore Gas & Electric Co. | 38.7 | 12.8 | 48.3 | 0.8 | 8.43 | 38.9 | 11.8 | 2.97 | 2.42 |
| Conowingo Power Co. | 100.0 | .0 | .0 | .0 | 3.02 | 100.0 | 8.3 | 88.17 | 34.24 |
| Potomac Edison Co., The | 39.5 | 12.2 | 48.1 | 0.2 | 8.57 | 44.6 | 9.5 | 2.88 | 2.35 |
| Susquehanna Electric Co. | 32.4 | .0 | 67.6 | .0 | 2.13 | 32.4 | | 6.77 | 1.00 |
| Susquehanna Power Co., The | 100.0 | .0 | .0 | .0 | .0 | 100.0 | 5.6 | .00 | .00 |
| **MASSACHUSETTS** | | | | | | | | | |
| Boston Edison Co. | 36.1 | 6.2 | 53.0 | 4.7 | 8.80 | 38.9 | 11.8 | 1.72 | 1.72 |
| Cambridge Electric Light Co. | 54.7 | .0 | 45.3 | .0 | 5.41 | 54.3 | 5.1 | 1.88 | 1.58 |
| Canal Electric Co. | 42.9 | .0 | 39.2 | 17.9 | 7.23 | 52.0 | 12.5 | 2.74 | 2.74 |
| Commonwealth Electric Co. | 53.1 | .0 | 46.9 | .0 | 6.58 | 52.9 | 6.9 | 1.30 | 1.30 |
| Eastern Edison Co. | 40.7 | 10.4 | 48.3 | 0.5 | 8.71 | 41.4 | 12.5 | 2.37 | 2.21 |
| Fitchburg Gas & Electric Light Co. | 33.1 | 7.2 | 40.4 | 19.4 | 10.47 | 38.8 | 14.4 | 1.79 | 1.70 |
| Holyoke Gas & Electric Co. | 73.8 | .0 | 26.2 | .0 | 3.72 | 73.4 | 4.0 | 4.57 | 3.25 |
| Holyoke Water Power Co. | 40.8 | .0 | 59.7 | .0 | 7.12 | 47.5 | 6.4 | 1.52 | 1.52 |
| Massachusetts Electric Co. | 36.5 | 18.4 | 51.1 | .0 | 7.83 | 34.7 | 17.5 | 4.16 | 2.91 |
| Montaup Electric Co. | 43.5 | .7 | 44.4 | 11.4 | 11.61 | 46.6 | 14.5 | 1.70 | 1.70 |
| Nantucket Electric Co. | 49.3 | .0 | 39.8 | 10.9 | 7.15 | 54.4 | 8.0 | 1.77 | 1.66 |
| New England Power Co. | 36.0 | 9.0 | 47.9 | 7.0 | 8.96 | 39.2 | 18.3 | 1.90 | 1.90 |
| Western Massachusetts Electric Co. | 31.9 | 10.4 | 55.8 | 1.9 | 8.77 | 34.0 | 11.5 | 1.74 | 1.64 |
| Yankee Atomic Electric Co. | 51.1 | .0 | 27.1 | 21.8 | 7.24 | 66.1 | 15.0 | 3.66 | 2.07 |

| | | | | | | | | | |
|---|---|---|---|---|---|---|---|---|---|
| **MICHIGAN** | | | | | | | | | |
| Alpena Power Co. | 51.2 | 12.4 | 14.5 | 21.8 | 6.87 | 60.0 | 4.4 | 1.92 | 1.58 |
| Consumers Power Co. | 36.2 | 8.9 | 48.0 | 7.0 | 9.85 | 38.5 | 9.5 | 1.78 | 1.78 |
| Detroit Edison Co., The | 33.8 | 9.1 | 52.9 | 4.2 | 10.05 | 35.6 | 10.2 | 1.74 | 1.73 |
| Edison Sault Electric Co. | 34.6 | 10.3 | 47.4 | 7.6 | 8.49 | 36.1 | 16.1 | 2.44 | 2.29 |
| Michigan Power Co. | 53.2 | .0 | 46.8 | .0 | 6.77 | 54.8 | 8.5 | 1.65 | 1.47 |
| Upper Peninsula Generating Co. | 21.3 | .0 | 67.9 | 10.8 | 8.13 | 23.4 | .0 | 1.01 | 1.01 |
| Upper Peninsula Power Co. | 31.9 | 11.2 | 57.0 | .0 | 8.72 | 33.3 | 11.7 | 2.18 | 1.86 |
| Cliffs Electric Service Co. | 54.4 | .0 | 45.6 | .0 | 139.58 | 51.5 | 11.7 | 3.37 | 2.58 |
| **MINNESOTA** | | | | | | | | | |
| Minnesota Power & Light Co. | 35.9 | 11.1 | 52.6 | 0.5 | 8.58 | 35.2 | 13.3 | 2.58 | 2.26 |
| Northern States Power Co. | 41.4 | 10.7 | 44.3 | 3.6 | 7.82 | 43.3 | 13.6 | 3.69 | 2.67 |
| **MISSISSIPPI** | | | | | | | | | |
| Mississippi Power Co. | 34.9 | 10.9 | 54.2 | .0 | 8.87 | 38.5 | 17.5 | 3.47 | 2.57 |
| Mississippi Power & Light Co. | 36.6 | 11.4 | 51.4 | 0.6 | 8.64 | 37.1 | 17.7 | 3.57 | 2.62 |
| **MISSOURI** | | | | | | | | | |
| Empire District Electric Co. | 34.8 | 11.7 | 50.3 | 3.2 | 7.10 | 35.5 | 8.9 | 1.93 | 1.84 |
| Kansas City Power & Light Co. | 38.4 | 12.0 | 48.1 | 6.5 | 9.09 | 35.5 | 14.8 | 2.26 | 2.15 |
| Missouri Edison Co. | 50.7 | .0 | 44.0 | 5.3 | 9.12 | 54.6 | 9.0 | 1.82 | 1.81 |
| Missouri Power & Light Co. | 36.3 | 5.3 | 56.1 | 2.3 | 7.72 | 36.5 | 9.6 | 1.88 | 1.71 |
| Missouri Public Service Co. | 31.8 | 12.8 | 51.0 | 4.5 | 9.05 | 32.0 | 16.7 | 2.19 | 2.19 |
| Missouri Utilities Co. | 34.2 | 4.5 | 57.1 | 4.2 | 8.08 | 37.0 | 7.1 | 1.40 | 1.40 |
| St. Joseph Light & Power Co. | 33.2 | 10.7 | 54.7 | 1.4 | 9.83 | 31.5 | 14.3 | 2.13 | 1.93 |
| Union Electric Co. | 35.4 | 11.6 | 49.5 | 3.4 | 7.87 | 37.0 | 11.6 | 1.88 | 1.88 |
| **MONTANA** | | | | | | | | | |
| Montana Power Co., The | 35.5 | 9.4 | 49.5 | 5.6 | 10.54 | 38.9 | 15.9 | 2.49 | 2.49 |
| **NEVADA** | | | | | | | | | |
| Nevada Power Co. | 35.8 | 10.1 | 48.3 | 5.8 | 11.46 | 39.3 | 16.1 | 2.49 | 2.26 |
| Sierra Pacific Power Co. | 34.1 | 12.0 | 46.5 | 7.4 | 8.87 | 36.4 | 10.2 | 1.97 | 1.85 |
| **NEW HAMPSHIRE** | | | | | | | | | |
| Concord Electric Co. | 42.8 | 8.7 | 43.5 | 5.0 | 9.05 | 44.8 | 12.0 | 2.48 | 2.27 |
| Connecticut Valley Electric Co. | 93.3 | .0 | 6.7 | .0 | 7.84 | 93.1 | 7.1 | 4.32 | 3.38 |
| Exeter & Hampton Electric Co. | 41.4 | 11.2 | 44.3 | 2.6 | 8.62 | 41.2 | 12.8 | 8.07 | 2.60 |
| Granite State Electric Co. | 56.4 | .0 | 43.6 | .0 | 6.78 | 54.7 | 7.1 | 1.66 | 1.63 |
| Public Service of New Hampshire | 38.8 | 18.9 | 36.9 | 10.3 | 9.25 | 42.0 | 18.5 | 2.06 | 2.03 |
| **NEW JERSEY** | | | | | | | | | |
| Atlantic City Electric Co. | 38.5 | 11.8 | 46.6 | 3.1 | 10.56 | 39.3 | 13.1 | 2.53 | 2.18 |
| Jersey Central Power & Light Co. | 37.6 | 11.8 | 50.5 | 0.5 | 6.72 | 87.9 | .- | 1.86 | 1.36 |
| Public Service Electric & Gas Co. | 41.2 | 11.4 | 43.5 | 3.8 | 8.81 | 42.2 | 9.8 | 2.35 | 2.32 |
| Rockland Electric Co. | 43.2 | 8.5 | 43.3 | .0 | 7.86 | 27.5 | 23.0 | 2.75 | 2.36 |
| **NEW MEXICO** | | | | | | | | | |
| New Mexico Electric Service Co. | 66.3 | 12.6 | 38.7 | 4.3 | 10.82 | 63.8 | 18.9 | 8.04 | 5.58 |
| Public Service Co. of New Mexico | 37.8 | — | 45.3 | — | 12.22 | 36.8 | 18.1 | 8.14 | 2.82 |

# Selected Financial Indicators—Continued

| Utilities | Capitalization Ratios [1] | | | | Rate of Return on Electric Utility Rate Base | Common Equity Percent of Total Capitalization [2] | Rate of Return on Common Equity | Interest Coverage Times Earned [3] | |
|---|---|---|---|---|---|---|---|---|---|
| | Common Equity | Preferred Stock | Long-Term Debt | Short-Term Debt (Notes Payable) | | | | Before Taxes | After Taxes |
| **NEW YORK** | | | | | | | | | |
| Central Hudson Gas & Electric Corp. | 37.9 | 11.7 | 47.2 | 3.2 | 10.26 | 38.1 | 18.8 | 2.29 | 2.07 |
| Con Edison Co. of N.Y., Inc. | 48.0 | 10.5 | 41.5 | - | 9.18 | 46.7 | 18.6 | 4.48 | 3.44 |
| Long Island Lighting Co. | 37.0 | 14.2 | 48.8 | - | 13.47 | 37.2 | 18.9 | 2.60 | 2.59 |
| Long Sault, Inc. | 100.0 | - | - | * | * | 100.0 | 5.8 | .00 | .00 |
| N.Y. State Electric & Gas Corp. | 38.7 | 13.2 | 46.2 | 1.9 | 10.98 | 38.9 | 18.2 | 2.47 | 2.39 |
| Niagara Mohawk Power Corp. | 39.6 | 12.9 | 44.1 | 3.4 | 8.16 | 40.2 | 18.5 | 2.52 | 2.47 |
| Orange & Rockland Utilities, Inc. | 44.2 | 13.4 | 40.7 | 1.7 | 8.66 | 43.9 | 18.1 | 3.16 | 2.72 |
| Rochester Gas & Electric Corp. | 41.9 | 11.3 | 46.8 | - | 9.42 | 53.7 | 18.1 | 2.65 | 2.57 |
| **NORTH CAROLINA** | | | | | | | | | |
| Carolina Power & Light Co. | 34.8 | 12.8 | 45.8 | 6.6 | 8.82 | 36.7 | 12.3 | 1.95 | 1.95 |
| Duke Power Co. | 37.5 | 12.6 | 46.8 | 3.1 | 6.65 | 37.7 | 13.7 | 2.41 | 2.32 |
| Nantahala Power & Light Co. | 52.9 | - | 47.1 | - | 6.31 | 51.8 | 8.2 | 2.68 | 2.03 |
| Yadkin, Inc. | 100.0 | - | - | - | 4.56 | 100.0 | 4.9 | .00 | .00 |
| **NORTH DAKOTA** | | | | | | | | | |
| Montana Dakota Utilities Co. | 40.7 | 11.8 | 44.8 | 2.7 | 7.68 | 40.5 | 13.3 | 2.02 | 2.02 |
| Otter Tail Power Co. | 31.8 | 14.7 | 46.0 | 7.5 | 7.32 | 33.6 | 7.6 | 1.72 | 1.71 |
| **OHIO** | | | | | | | | | |
| Cincinnati Gas & Electric Co., Inc. | 33.8 | 13.8 | 50.4 | 2.5 | 8.61 | 34.6 | 11.9 | 2.08 | 2.08 |
| Cleveland Electric Illuminating Co., Inc. | 34.9 | 14.7 | 47.0 | 3.3 | 9.23 | 36.4 | 12.7 | 2.13 | 2.07 |
| Columbus & So. Ohio Electric Co. | 35.8 | 12.0 | 50.3 | 1.9 | 10.45 | 36.3 | 12.0 | 2.10 | 2.07 |
| Dayton Power & Light Co., The | 34.4 | 13.3 | 48.6 | 3.7 | 10.91 | 35.2 | 14.1 | 2.34 | 2.28 |
| Ohio Edison Co. | 33.2 | 10.5 | 54.6 | 1.7 | 10.23 | 33.4 | 14.3 | 1.85 | 1.85 |
| Ohio Power Co. | 31.7 | 10.4 | 53.5 | 4.4 | 9.93 | 32.8 | 12.9 | 2.02 | 1.98 |
| Ohio Valley Electric Corp. | 12.0 | - | 76.2 | 11.8 | 4.95 | 11.3 | 15.7 | 1.39 | 1.25 |
| Toledo Edison Co., The | 33.8 | 15.1 | 49.7 | 1.4 | 9.34 | 34.1 | 13.6 | 2.08 | 1.98 |
| **OKLAHOMA** | | | | | | | | | |
| Oklahoma Gas & Electric Co. | 39.6 | 11.2 | 49.2 | .0 | 8.34 | 38.5 | 12.4 | 2.53 | 2.21 |
| Public Service Co. of Oklahoma | 45.3 | 7.0 | 47.7 | .0 | 8.01 | 44.3 | 12.2 | 1.67 | 2.14 |
| **OREGON** | | | | | | | | | |
| CP National | 36.5 | 6.5 | 44.3 | 12.7 | 10.72 | 38.9 | 14.9 | 1.84 | 1.84 |
| Pacific Power & Light Co. | 37.6 | 11.8 | 47.4 | 3.1 | 8.93 | 39.2 | 13.3 | 2.16 | 2.18 |
| Portland General Electric Co. | 34.9 | 7.3 | 56.8 | 0.9 | 11.63 | 35.2 | 14.9 | 1.91 | 1.86 |

| | | | | | | | | | |
|---|---|---|---|---|---|---|---|---|---|
| **PENNSYLVANIA** | | | | | | | | | |
| Citizens' Electric Co. | 100.0 | .0 | .0 | .0 | 11.05 | 100.0 | 13.7 | .00 | .00 |
| Duquesne Light Co. | 42.6 | 4.9 | 52.5 | .0 | 8.62 | 43.0 | 9.3 | 2.24 | 2.05 |
| Metropolitan Edison Co. | 34.5 | 12.9 | 51.1 | 1.5 | 3.33 | 35.0 | .8 | 0.96 | 0.94 |
| Pennsylvania Electric Co. | 33.2 | 13.2 | 53.6 | .0 | 6.71 | 33.0 | 8.3 | 1.96 | 1.78 |
| Pennsylvania Power Co. | 35.9 | 12.7 | 49.4 | 2.1 | 9.20 | 35.9 | 10.6 | 1.89 | 1.93 |
| Pennsylvania Power & Light Co. | 31.5 | 17.0 | 47.6 | 3.9 | 8.81 | 32.8 | 13.6 | 2.00 | 1.97 |
| Philadelphia Electric Co. | 36.2 | 11.8 | 51.0 | 0.9 | 9.38 | 36.1 | 12.1 | 2.06 | 1.93 |
| Pike County Light & Power Co. | 60.5 | .0 | 39.5 | .0 | 1.58 | 60.9 | 4.6 | 0.61 | 0.38 |
| Safe Harbor Water Power Co. | 69.2 | .0 | 29.0 | 1.7 | 8.47 | 69.9 | 9.7 | 8.79 | 4.99 |
| UGI Corp. | 43.2 | 11.2 | 43.2 | 2.4 | 8.49 | 43.4 | 15.3 | 3.02 | 2.53 |
| West Penn Power Co. | 38.6 | 12.2 | 48.0 | 1.2 | 9.95 | 38.6 | 17.2 | 3.70 | 2.94 |
| York Haven Power Co. | 100.0 | .0 | .0 | .0 | 10.07 | 100.0 | 9.8 | 56.02 | 31.23 |
| **RHODE ISLAND** | | | | | | | | | |
| Blackstone Valley Electric Co. | 31.1 | 11.5 | 57.4 | .0 | 11.69 | 30.4 | 8.9 | 1.70 | 1.38 |
| Narragansett Electric Co. | 35.6 | 14.6 | 49.8 | .0 | 7.90 | 35.6 | 13.2 | 3.07 | 2.27 |
| Newport Electric Corp. | 27.7 | 8.5 | 63.8 | .0 | 8.61 | 25.5 | 5.6 | 1.28 | 1.28 |
| **SOUTH CAROLINA** | | | | | | | | | |
| Lockhart Power Co. | 100.0 | .0 | .0 | .0 | 5.19 | 100.0 | 6.6 | 20.73 | 20.73 |
| So. Carolina Electric & Gas Co. | 34.9 | 10.6 | 53.1 | 1.5 | 11.05 | 34.6 | 13.2 | 2.06 | 1.91 |
| **SOUTH DAKOTA** | | | | | | | | | |
| Black Hills Power & Light Co. | 53.3 | 11.9 | 34.7 | .0 | 7.50 | 52.0 | 16.1 | 4.38 | 4.05 |
| Northwestern Public Service Co. | 31.1 | 11.1 | 54.5 | 3.4 | 8.64 | 31.6 | 11.7 | 1.85 | 1.82 |
| **TENNESSEE** | | | | | | | | | |
| Kingsport Power Co. | 38.5 | .0 | 61.5 | .0 | 7.87 | 38.6 | 4.7- | 0.78 | 0.78 |
| Tapoco, Inc. | 100.0 | .0 | .0 | .0 | 4.69 | 100.0 | 3.8 | .00 | .00 |
| **TEXAS** | | | | | | | | | |
| Central Power & Light Co. | 43.6 | 10.5 | 45.9 | .0 | 9.92 | 43.2 | 16.0 | 3.15 | 2.75 |
| Dallas Power & Light Co. | 47.8 | 10.8 | 41.4 | .0 | 12.65 | 48.4 | 16.0 | 4.08 | 3.23 |
| El Paso Electric Co. | 37.8 | 10.8 | 36.3 | 15.0 | 18.23 | 44.2 | 19.4 | 2.57 | 2.43 |
| Houston Lighting & Power Co. | 45.4 | 6.5 | 47.5 | 0.6 | 10.55 | 45.2 | 14.3 | 2.88 | 2.60 |
| Southwestern Electric Power Co. | 37.9 | 10.6 | 51.5 | .0 | 9.89 | 40.2 | 15.5 | 2.91 | 2.51 |
| Southwestern Electric Service Co. | 42.1 | 5.9 | 52.0 | .0 | 8.26 | 41.9 | 12.1 | 2.49 | 2.18 |
| Southwestern Public Service Co. | 34.1 | 11.1 | 52.2 | 2.6 | 9.32 | 34.7 | 16.9 | 2.37 | 2.37 |
| Texas Electric Service Co. | 46.6 | 11.8 | 41.5 | 8.5 | 14.18 | 45.3 | 18.1 | 4.13 | 3.33 |
| Texas - New Mexico Service Co. | 38.7 | 6.9 | 47.9 | 0.1 | 8.61 | 39.1 | 9.6 | 1.54 | 1.54 |
| Texas Power & Light Co. | 43.3 | 11.6 | 45.0 | .0 | 11.21 | 42.5 | 16.0 | 3.66 | 3.03 |
| West Texas Utilities Co. | 48.2 | 3.0 | 48.9 | .0 | 7.10 | 47.4 | 11.6 | 2.59 | 2.20 |
| **UTAH** | | | | | | | | | |
| Utah Power & Light Co. | 40.0 | 10.8 | 49.1 | .0 | 9.10 | 40.3 | 11.8 | 2.39 | 2.30 |
| **VERMONT** | | | | | | | | | |
| Central Vermont Public Service Co. | 37.3 | 13.5 | 45.2 | 4.0 | 14.45 | 46.6 | 13.6 | 2.42 | 2.42 |
| Green Mountain Power Corp. | 27.8 | 6.2 | 39.1 | 26.9 | 16.12 | 36.5 | 10.5 | 1.66 | 1.65 |
| Vermont Electric Power Co., Inc. | 9.9 | .0 | 79.9 | 10.2 | 8.34 | 10.8 | 7.6 | 1.15 | 1.10 |
| Vermont Yankee Nuclear Power Corp. | 35.6 | 10.5 | 53.9 | .0 | 5.51 | 36.3 | 10.5 | 2.00 | 1.75 |

# Selected Financial Indicators—Continued

| Utilities | Capitalization Ratios [1] | | | | Rate of Return on Electric Utility Rate Base | Common Equity Percent of Total Capital- ization [2] | Rate of Return on Common Equity | Interest Coverage Times Earned | |
|---|---|---|---|---|---|---|---|---|---|
| | Common Equity | Preferred Stock | Long-Term Debt | Short-Term Debt (Notes Payable) | | | | Before Taxes | After Taxes |
| **VIRGINIA** | | | | | | | | | |
| Old Dominion Power Co. | 22.6 | .0 | 77.4 | .0 | 7.09 | 24.7 | .3 | 0.54 | 0.54 |
| Virginia Electric & Power Co. | 32.3 | 11.2 | 53.8 | 2.7 | 10.13 | 33.4 | 9.5 | 1.81 | 1.74 |
| **WASHINGTON** | | | | | | | | | |
| Puget Sound Power & Light Co. | 36.2 | 9.3 | 52.0 | 2.5 | 12.09 | 37.8 | 16.6 | 2.33 | 2.28 |
| Washington Water Power Co., The | 39.5 | 8.9 | 51.6 | .0 | 10.93 | 39.1 | 13.7 | 2.49 | 2.33 |
| **WEST VIRGINIA** | | | | | | | | | |
| Appalachian Power Co. | 35.1 | 9.0 | 53.6 | 2.3 | 10.69 | 36.0 | 14.4 | 2.07 | 2.03 |
| Monongahela Power Co. | 37.7 | 13.3 | 49.0 | .0 | 8.79 | 37.4 | 12.6 | 2.75 | 2.33 |
| Wheeling Electric Co. | 41.7 | .0 | 58.3 | .0 | 13.69 | 42.2 | 8.6 | 1.25 | 1.25 |
| **WISCONSIN** | | | | | | | | | |
| Consolidated Water Power Co. | 100.0 | .0 | .0 | .0 | .92 | 100.0 | 0.2 | .00 | .00 |
| Lake Superior District Power Co. | 45.1 | 6.7 | 40.5 | 7.7 | 8.73 | 47.7 | 8.5 | 2.47 | 1.82 |
| Madison Gas & Power Co. | 42.9 | 12.7 | 39.4 | 5.1 | 9.24 | 44.7 | 9.2 | 3.17 | 2.40 |
| Northern States Power Co. | 68.1 | .0 | 31.9 | .0 | 9.67 | 68.0 | 7.7 | 2.97 | 1.89 |
| Northwestern Wisconsin Electric Co. | 37.9 | .0 | 31.2 | 30.9 | 10.59 | 49.4 | 9.5 | 1.52 | 1.48 |
| Superior Water Light & Power Co. | 47.3 | .0 | 47.8 | 4.9 | 11.46 | 50.0 | 9.4 | 2.27 | 1.82 |
| Wisconsin Electric Power Co. | 42.1 | 11.3 | 45.7 | .0 | 10.96 | 41.3 | 13.7 | 3.03 | 2.46 |
| Wisconsin Power & Light Co. | 39.9 | 11.0 | 49.1 | .0 | 11.33 | 40.4 | 14.5 | 3.38 | 2.39 |
| Wisconsin Public Service Corp. | 39.0 | 12.0 | 41.9 | 7.2 | 8.94 | 42.4 | 13.8 | 2.80 | 2.43 |
| Wisconsin River Power Co. | 92.2 | .0 | 7.8 | .0 | 2.13[2] | 91.0 | 1.2 | 2.29 | 2.12 |
| **WYOMING** | | | | | | | | | |
| Cheyenne Light Fuel & Power Co. | 40.8 | .0 | 31.0 | 28.2 | 8.43 | 55.3 | 11.5 | 1.70 | 1.70 |

[1] Includes short-term debt (notes payable) as a part of total capitalization.
[2] Excludes short-term debt (notes payable) as a part of total capitalization.
NM = Not Meaningful
Note: Totals may not equal sum of components due to independent rounding.

SOURCE: Energy Information Administration, "Statistics of Privately Owned Electric Utilities, 1981 Annual," June 1983.

## APPENDIX C

### Leading Utilities in Load Reductions through 1992 as a Result of Conservation and Load Management Programs

| Company | Generating Capacity 1982 | Projected Annual Increase in Demand through 1982 | Program Costs in 1982 (000) | Projected MWs Saved through 1992 |
|---|---|---|---|---|
| TVA | 32,076 | 2.38 | 57,000 | 4,000 |
| Duke Power | 14,526 | 3.87 | NA | 2,994 |
| Florida P&L | 12,865 | 3.5 | 23,000 | 2,100 |
| Pacific G&E | 16,319 | 0.9 | 84,000 | 1,871 |
| Carolina P&L | 8,085 | 3.0 | 10,600 | 1,750 |
| Houston L&P | 12,966 | 2.6 | 12,500 | 1,700 |
| So Calif Ed | 15,345 | 2.0 | 46,154 | 1,500 |
| Florida Power | 5,899 | 1.0 | 5,000 | 1,500 |
| Public Service E&G | 9,023 | 1.3 | 9,000 | 956 |
| BPA | 0 | NA | 86,000 | 802 |
| Jersey Central P&L | 3,371 | 1.5 | 9,000 | 800 |
| Alabama Power | 9,194 | 2.59 | 1,266 | 800 |
| Penn Electric | 2,736 | 2.0 | 4,200 | 671 |
| Los Angeles | 6,749 | 1.7 | 7,876 | 601 |
| Oklahoma G&E | 5,359 | NA | NA | 600 |
| Northern States | 6,162 | 2.0 | 10,000 | 600 |
| Metropolitan Ed | 2,144 | 1.85 | 1,000 | 485 |
| Texas P&L | 7,904 | 5.1 | 5,100 | 465 |
| Detroit Ed | 9,458 | 2.5 | 13,000 | 450 |
| Arizona PSC | 3,522 | 2.3 | 3,230 | 420 |
| Kansas City P&L | 2,774 | 2.3 | NA | 412 |
| Tampa Electric | 2,495 | 2.7 | 8,000 | 400 |
| Penn P&L | 6,470 | 1.5 | 4,700 | 390 |
| Consolidated Ed | 10,564 | 1.0 | 440 | 370 |
| Utah P&L | 2,751 | NA | 10,440 | 318 |

SOURCE: IRRC survey.

## APPENDIX D

### Leading Utilities in Purchases of
### Third-Party Power Production through 1992
(capacity in megawatts)

| Company | Purchased Capacity in 1982 | Estimated Additional Capacity by 1992 | Total Capacity Purchases, 1992 |
|---|---|---|---|
| Houston Lighting & Power | 1,000 | 1,400 | 2,400 |
| Pacific Gas & Electric | 259 | 2,100 | 2,359 |
| Southern California Edison | 195 | 1,000 | 1,195 |
| Virginia Electric & Power | 566 | 368 | 934 |
| Gulf States | 0 | 600 | 600 |
| Carolina Power & Light | 241 | 257 | 498 |
| TVA | 110 | 300 | 410 |
| Georgia Power | 350 | NA | 350 |
| Florida Power | 38 | 277 | 315 |
| New England Electric | 65 | 173 | 238 |
| Long Island Lighting | 1 | 230 | 231 |
| Pacific Power & Light | 10 | 204 | 214 |
| Los Angeles | 66 | 120 | 186 |
| Philadelphia Electric | 1 | 180 | 181 |
| Florida Power & Light | 89 | 80 | 169 |
| Central Maine Power | 75 | 80 | 155 |
| Hawaiian Electric | 28 | 125 | 153 |
| Idaho Power | 1 | 135 | 136 |
| San Diego Gas & Electric | 0 | 135 | 135 |
| Penn Electric | 62 | 70 | 132 |
| PSC of New Hampshire | 38 | 78 | 116 |
| Detroit Edison | 6 | 100 | 106 |
| Wisconsin Electric | 2 | 101 | 103 |
| Sierra Pacific | 1 | 100 | 101 |

SOURCE: IRRC survey.

# ABOUT THE AUTHOR

SCOTT A. FENN is energy program director and treasurer at the Investor Responsibility Research Center, a Washington, D.C.-based registered investment advisor. He has also served as a contributor to the Network News/UPI national press syndicate.

Mr. Fenn is the author of <u>Energy Conservation By Industry</u> (IRRC, 1979), <u>The Nuclear Power Debate: Issues and Choices</u> (Praeger, 1981), and some 50 articles and research reports on various energy topics.

Mr. Fenn is a native of Minneapolis, Minnesota, and holds a B.A. in economics from Williams College.